POWER MATES

ESSENTIAL CHECKMATING STRATEGIES AND TECHNIQUES

BRUCE PANDOLFINI

A Fireside Book
PUBLISHED BY SIMON & SCHUSTER

FIRESIDE
Rockefeller Center
1230 Avenue of the Americas
New York, NY 10020

FIRESIDE and colophon are registered trademarks
of Simon & Schuster Inc.

Designed by Stanley S. Drate/Folio Graphics Co. Inc.

Manufactured in the United States of America

3   5   7   9   10   8   6   4   2

Library of Congress Cataloging-in-Publication Data

Pandolfini, Bruce.
    Power mates : essential checkmating strategies and techniques /
Bruce Pandolfini.
            p.   cm.
        "A Fireside book."
        Includes index.
        1. Checkmate (Chess)   I. Title.
        GV1450.7.P456   1996
        794.1'24—dc20   96-33582
                                                              CIP

ISBN 0-684-80120-5

for Bruce Alberston,
a great teacher and a true friend

Acknowledgments

The creation of a chess book requires the efforts of many people. Players, analysts, fact checkers, diagrammers, indexers, programmers, editors, production staff and others join forces with the writer to fashion a new text. In my own case, I must especially thank Bruce Alberston, Holly Cannell, Sydney Cohen, Sam Cross, Leslie Ellen, Deirdre Hare, Ellen Kantor, Chris Reid, Chris Shea, Fred Wilson, Rob Henderson, and Diana Newman. Each improved the text with a personal stamp.

CONTENTS

INTRODUCTION

There was a special reason for writing this book: to add a chapter to my own teaching materials. I wished to focus on students who already play chess and want to sharpen their game. They require a more advanced approach than rank beginners.

What do these students need to learn? They've absorbed the moves and rules, the object of the game, a few basics, and one or two simple openings. Now they're on their way, ready to travel the bumpy road to checkmate, along all its divergent paths—not just the mating positions, but many of the standard ways they're brought about. Knowing multifarious checkmate setups is important, but abstractions can take you just so far. In order to understand the winning process, it's better to meet up with typical attacks and patterns in actual chess games, where mate is the natural outcome of logical play.

Among the various types of games one can study, I prefer the short, modern kind. They're easier to follow, tactically aggressive, and freshly appealing. Games that focus on positional themes, on the other hand, tend to be subtle and complex. Such matchups, too long for most students to analyze and study conveniently, fail didactically.

Short new games are also preferable for teaching because most students are excited by what's innovative and different. These games are more likely to be germane to your own encounters, it not being unusual for your opponents to try out lines and variations they've seen in current magazines and in their own tournaments. Why study obsolescent illustrations already known to everyone and not likely to happen in your own contests? However worthy such older examples might be, surprise is the key, and today's players, events, and openings are what it's all about.

There's a group of teachers who advocate initially studying the ending over the beginning. Though this philosophy has merit, I see chess as a more harmonized concept, where start and finish meld together. I believe you can study one to study all, and it's this integrated approach I've tried to give to the volume at hand.

Short games stress openings, where expertise stands out. Strong chessplayers are confident because they know where to go from the start, equipped to attack and defend against all the usual beginning moves. Thus, for optimal effectiveness, I believe a collection of chess games should be arranged to provide greater access to particular opening variations. Furthermore, since checkmate is often a direct consequence of early moves and developments, organizing the examples by the branch opening that generates them reinforces the wholeness of the game and the correlation between its parts.

First and foremost, *Power Mates* is a collection of 70 short contemporary chess games, every one terminating in 25 moves or less. In each case, the loser is either mated or chooses to resign because mate is certain. An added feature is that many of the games are between first-class players— even some world champions. The annotations are moderate, just a few explanations to clarify the text. And in storyboard fashion, each game is illustrated by four captioned diagrams. With so many "pictures," it almost becomes possible to follow the games without using a chessboard. I've made the text this visual because I think chess ideas are assimilated faster when seen. To increase practicality, the last diagram of each game is a problem accompanied by a question, the answer being a forced checkmate. *Power Mates* thereby functions as a puzzle book, encapsulating 70 mating tasks, with the answers appearing in a separate section.

Finally, as indicated earlier, *Power Mates* presents all the games by opening according to their ECO (Encyclopedia of the Chess Openings) code; symbols used internationally to identify openings by a letter (A to E) and numbers (1 to 99). The popular Sicilian Defense, for instance, is classified anywhere from B20 to B99, depending on the particular sub-variation.

As for the games, each one begins with a summary paragraph underscoring themes and key points. These are short narratives highlighting correct actions and pointing out violations of principle. Then comes the game, the moves presented vertically down the page in boldface algebraic notation. Reasons and suggestions appear throughout, chaperoning the lines of symbols with verbal elucidations. The moves of the variations in the notes are given in ordinary type, thus distinguishing actual moves (boldface) from mere analysis. As already indicated, each game concludes with a problem, to determine the actual winning moves. Answers can be found in the back of *Power Mates*, along with indexes to make reading this volume easier and more useful.

All in all, *Power Mates* is an up-to-date checkmate treatise, based on how it's done today. It's also a manual of openings, a quiz book, and a vivid collection of contemporary attack in chess, showing what advancing players need to know and how they get there. I might even use it for my own students.

How to Read Chess Moves in Algebraic Notation

Power Mates uses algebraic chess notation to convey moves. To understand algebraic notation you must view the chessboard as an eight-by-eight grid. Every square on the grid has its own name, based on the intersecting file and rank.

Files, the rows of squares going up and down, are lettered **a** through **h**. Ranks, the rows of squares going across, are numbered 1 through 8.

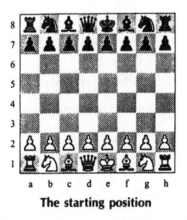

The starting position

Squares are designated by combining those letters and numbers. For each name, the letter is lowercase and appears first, before the number. Thus, in the diagram of the starting position, White's queen occupies **d1** and Black's **d8.**

There is only one perspective in the algebraic system: White's. All squares are named from White's side of the board. For example, the a-file is always on White's left and

Black's right. The first rank is always the one closest to White and farthest from Black.

The algebraic grid below gives the names and positions of all the squares. You might find it helpful to photocopy it and use it as a bookmark so it's always there as a reminder.

BLACK

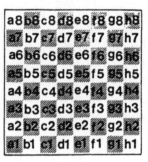

WHITE

The algebraic grid. Every square has a unique name.

Other Symbols

You should also familarize yourself with the following symbols:

Symbol	Meaning
K	king
Q	queen
R	rook
B	bishop
N	knight
P	pawn (not used in algebraic notation)
–	moves to
x	captures
+	check
#	checkmate

0–0	castles kingside
0–0–0	castles queenside
!	good move
?	bad move
!!	brilliant move
??	blunder
!?	probably a good move
?!	probably a bad move
e.p.	en passant
1-0	White wins
0-1	Black wins

Note that though **P** stands for pawn, it is not used in algebraic notation (though it is used in descriptive notation, which is not necessary for this book). If no indication of the moving unit is given in algebraic notation, the move is a pawn move.

POWER GAME **1**

Dobosz vs. Bednarski
Esbjerg, 1979

White wastes time, moving his queen too early and neglecting kingside development. Black counters by advancing the d-pawn, taking advantage of an e-file pin. Suddenly, Black sacrifices a knight, forcing the king to take, and White loses the right to castle. A furious chase ensues, impelled by sharp tactics. The white king is hunted up the board and finally mated in a criss-cross.

Polish Opening A00

1.	b4	e5
2.	Bb2	Bxb4

The trade of e-pawn for b-pawn benefits Black in this situation. His pieces activate quickly and, after castling kingside, he can station his rook on the e-file to plague White's king.

3.	Bxe5	Nf6
4.	Nf3	0-0
5.	e3	Re8
6.	c4	d5
7.	Qb3	. . .

White doesn't get much value out of this queen move, which neglects development. It would be better to leave the queen at home and develop the king-bishop, preparing to castle.

7.	. . .	Nc6
8.	Bb2	. . .

After White's 8th move

8.	...	d4!

Introducing tension in the center and seizing the initiative. White can't safely capture on d4 because of the pin along the e-file.

9.	Be2	...

On 9. Nxd4?, Black counters with 9. . . . Nxd4, when 10. Qxb4 meets with 10. . . . Nc2+, forking king and queen. And if 10. Bxd4, Black has the safe capture 10. . . . Qxd4, the e-pawn being pinned.

9.	...	dxe3
10.	fxe3	Ne4
11.	Nc3?	...

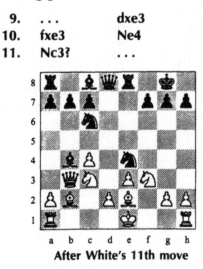

After White's 11th move

If 11. 0-0?, White drops the d-pawn for starters, but even after the text d2 remains vulnerable.

	11.	**...**	**Nxd2!**

This undermine's e3 and obliterates the middle pawn shields. White's king is still in the woods.

	12.	**Nxd2**	**Rxe3**

Threatening 13. . . . Nd4, along with 14. . . . Bxc3, removing the defender, and the e2-bishop hangs.

	13.	**Nf3**	**...**

The defensive 13. Nf1? doesn't help, for Black reverses the tactical order and still scores: 13. . . . Rxe2 +! 14. Kxe2 Nd4 +, forking king and queen.

	13.	**...**	**Bg4**

Intending 14. . . . Bxf3 and 15. . . . Nd4. White's king must abandon ship. Bring on Queequeg's coffin.

	14.	**Kf2**	**Bxf3!**
	15.	**Bxf3**	**...**

White drops the queen with 15. Kxe3 Bc5 + 16. Kxf3 Nd4 +, another fork. And if 15. gxf3, 15. . . . Qh4 + 16. Kxe3 Qd4# is a punishing mate.

	15.	**...**	**Qd2 +**

Forcing the king out to open sea, and the hunt starts.

	16.	**Kg3**	**...**

Retreating to g1 results in mate after 16. . . . Re1 +, or 16. . . . Rxf3, or 16. . . . Bc5. Nor does 16. Kf1 achieve more since 16. . . . Rae8 menaces mate at e1.

	16.	**...**	**Bd6 +**
	17.	**Kh3**	**...**

After White's 17th move

| 17. | ... | **Rxc3!** |

Clearing the c1-h6 diagonal for queen use.

| 18. | **Qxc3** | ... |

Now it's White's turn to threaten mate, but it's Black whose mate threat is implemented on move 20 (**0-1**).

Power Mate 1

Q1: How does Black mate in three moves?

POWER GAME *2*

Larsen vs. Spassky
Belgrade, 1970

Black takes back away from the middle to facilitate development, building up along the central files. He presses the attack to the kingside with the h-pawn. Black lets his knight hang to open the rook-file, then offers a rook to gain time. His queen invades, threatening promotion, and mate is meted out with the support of queen and bishop. One of the most famous games of the twentieth century.

Nimzovich/Larsen Opening A01

1.	b3	e5
2.	Bb2	Nc6
3.	c4	Nf6
4.	Nf3	. . .

Larsen plays to provoke the advance of the e5-pawn, hoping to target it later. In a subsequent game against Spassky (playing Black) later that same year, the great Dane opted for the conservative 4. e3.

4.	. . .	e4
5.	Nd4	Bc5
6.	Nxc6	dxc6

Better than 6. . . . bxc6, capturing toward the center, because it expedites rapid development. Spassky's opening scheme is entirely unpretentious. He just gets his pieces out and takes over the d-file.

7.	e3	Bf5
8.	Qc2	Qe7
9.	Be2	0-0-0
10.	f4?	. . .

After White's 10th move

Larsen plans 11. Bxf6 Qxf6 12. Nc3, aiming at the e-pawn. But before surrendering the dark-square bishop, he wants to insure control of e5. The drawbacks to moving the f-pawn are a weakened e3 and a vulnerable e1-h4 diagonal.

> **10.   ...   Ng4!**

Sidestepping White's plan and intending a queen check at h4. And if White blocks the check by 12. g3, then 12. . . . Qh3 menaces the kingside.

> **11.   g3   ...**

Greedily taking the pawn, 11. Bxg7 Rhg8 12. Bc3, doesn't work out so well. One fantasy continuation is 12. . . . Nxe3 13. dxe3 Qh4+ 14. g3 Rxg3 15. hxg3 Qxh1+ 16. Kf2 Bxe3+ 17. Kxe3 Qg1#. Larsen's move tries to stop the incursion Qe7-h4.

> **11.   ...   h5!**

Immediately focusing on the soft spot, the g3-pawn, even if it means throwing the g4-knight to the war dogs.

> **12.   h3   ...**

On 12. Nc3, there follows 12. . . . Rxd2!, when 13. Qxd2 is met by 13. . . . Bxe3 14. Qc2 Bf2+ and 15. . . . Ne3+, forking king and queen.

> **12.   ...   h4!**

After Black's 12th move

Achilles and Hector would be proud.

| 13. | hxg4 | ... |

A similar line ensues on 13. Bxg4 Bxg4 14. hxg4. Spassky gives 14. . . . hxg3 15. Rg1 Rh1! 16. Rxh1 g2 (to clear the e1-h4 diagonal with gain of time) 17. Rg1 Qh4+ 18. Ke2 Qxg4+ 19. Ke1 Qg3+ 20. Ke2 Qf3+ 21. Ke1 Be7! as winning for Black. And on 20. Kd1, Spassky offers 20. . . . Qf2 21. Qxe4 Qxg1+ 22. Kc2 Qf2 with decisive advantage.

| 13. | ... | hxg3 |
| 14. | Rg1 | ... |

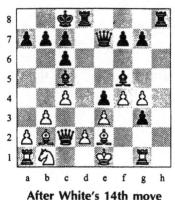

After White's 14th move

| 14. | ... | Rh1!! |

This is the move that makes the combination click. Spassky spent 17 minutes checking the variations before playing it on the board. The idea is to get the queen to h4 with tempo.

15.	Rxh1	g2
16.	Rf1	...

The main line, 16. Rg1, is no better: 16. . . . Qh4+ 17. Kd1 Qh1 18. Qc3 Qxg1+ 19. Kc2 Qf2 20. gxf5 Qxe2 21. Na3 Bb4!, when 22. Qxb4 is answered by 22. . . . Qd3+, promoting with checkmate.

16.	...	Qh4+
17.	Kd1	gxf1/Q+

White resigns (0-1).

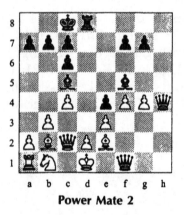

Power Mate 2

Q2: After the natural 18. Bxf1, how does Black mate?

POWER GAME 3

I. Sokolov vs. Tseshkovsky
Wijk ann Zee, 1989

Black initiates a pawn advance and his opponent ignores its menace. White's forces are driven back. Black invades on the forsaken kingside squares, disregarding threats to his own battalions, and breaks through. White's king is checked over to the queenside, where it meets inexorable mate.

English Opening A20

1.	c4	e5
2.	g3	d6
3.	Bg2	g6
4.	e3	. . .

This is a bit slow and somewhat weakens f3. The standard reaction to g7-g6 is an immediate d2-d4.

4.	. . .	Bg7
5.	Ne2	h5!?

An intriguing conception. The central formation (pawn on e5 vs. pawn on e3) already gives Black a slight spatial edge. With the text, he looks to gain even more *Lebensraum* by getting his pawn to h4, assailing g3 and possibly threatening h4-h3.

6.	d4?!	. . .

Countering a flank advance with a central thrust is nothing unusual. The problem is that Black's e5-pawn is securely defended. White instead might have tried 6. h4, halting the h5-pawn in its tracks, or 6. h3, retaining fighting rights to g4.

6.	. . .	h4!

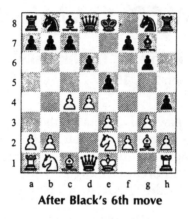

After Black's 6th move

7.	Nbc3	Nh6
8.	e4	...

Hoping to retain lost ground, but he assumes too many commitments.

8.	...	Bg4

Pins the knight and threatens to win the d4-pawn. Also retains an option on the pronged advance h4-h3, forcing the bishop to retreat to f1, with the follow-up intrusion Bg4-f3 in the air.

9.	Qd3	Nd7
10.	d5	Nc5

White has ceded control of the game to Black's gamboling forces.

11.	Qe3	h3
12.	Bf1	f5

Threatens 13. . . . fxe4 14. Nxe4 Nf5, winning a piece, for White's queen must abandon the defense of e4.

13.	f3	...

After White's 13th move

| 13. | ... | fxe4! |
| 14. | fxg4? | ... |

White should have swallowed his pride, instead of the poisoned g4-bishop, with 14. fxe4. Now the attack rolls unabated.

| 14. | ... | Nxg4 |

Here come the knights, along with their friends, the queen and the dark-square bishop.

| 15. | Qg1 | ... |

Her Majesty is stuck for squares: 15. Qg5 Nd3+ 16. Kd1 (16. Kd2 Qxg5+) 16. ... Qxg5 17. Bxg5 Nf2+ does disgraceful things to the h1-rook; and if 15. Qd2, then 15. ... Bh6 16. Qc2 Nd3+ 17. Kd1 Ngf2 is mate.

| 15. | ... | Qf6 |

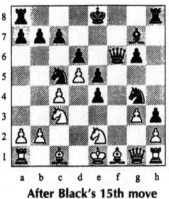

After Black's 15th move

There's no need to rush, for Nc5-d3+ won't run away. So
Black brings up the heavy artillery.

16.	Nd1	Nd3 +
17.	Kd2	. . .

Now King Lear must fend for himself.

17.	. . .	Qf3

If 18. Nec3, then 18. . . . Nb4 stops the king from fleeing
and sets up mate by 19. . . . Bh6+ 20. Ke1 Nc2#.

18.	a3	Bh6 +
19.	Kc2	. . .

Black played his 19th move and White resigned (0-1).

Power Mate 3

Q3: How does Black expedite mate?

POWER GAME **4**

Stean vs. Sax
Amsterdam, 1979

Black advances the f-pawn to activate the castled rook, while White fumbles his own strategy by castling into a major offensive. With White's queen out of play on the queenside, Black busts up White's kingside and invades on the accessible squares. The queen tries to get back, but Black obstructs retreat, and White's king, surrounded by hostile forces, is Waterlooed. Kaput!

English Opening A27

1.	Nf3	Nc6
2.	c4	e5
3.	Nc3	f5
4.	d4	e4
5.	Bg5	Be7
6.	Bxe7	Ncxe7

After Black's 6th move

There are four ways to capture on e7, and this is considered best. Black's way of taking back provides support for a subsequent c7-c6 and d7-d5, fighting for a share of the center.

	7.	Nd2	...

The blunder 7. Ne5? loses a retreatless knight to 7. . . . d7-d6.

7.	...	Nf6
8.	e3	0-0
9.	Be2	c6

Sax's new move is an improvement over the slower and less assertive d7-d6. Black plans to advance the d-pawn two squares.

10.	c5	d5
11.	cxd6 e.p.	Qxd6
12.	Nc4	Qc7
13.	Qb3	Be6

This development counters any discoveries on the a2-g8 diagonal, while also threatening 14. . . . b5, humiliating the pinned c4-knight.

14.	Qa3	Bxc4
15.	Bxc4 +	Kh8

After Black's 15th move

16.   0-0?   ...

A case of premature castling on move 16. There's more resistance in 16. g3, deterring f5-f4. The position of White's
king on the kingside is dubious with his queen bivouacked
on the queenside.

16.   ...   Ng6
17.   Be2   ...

Situating the bishop for defense by guarding some potential
kingside invasion points. If 17. g3, Black could reply 17. . . .
h5 with malice.

17.   ...   f4

Black is picking up space on the kingside. Now f4-f3 looms,
and White's queen is bogged down in a Russian winter, thou-
sands of miles away.

18.   Rae1?   ...

White can find more resilience in 18. Qc5 Rae8 19. Qg5,
transferring the queen to the kingside. White has this in
mind, but the one-move delay proves costly, and the queen
never gets back to Paris.

18.   ...   Qd7!

Black wants to transport his queen to h3. White needs to
teleport his.

19.   Qc5   ...

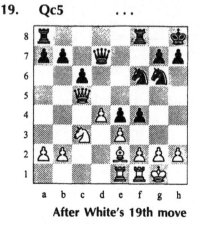

After White's 19th move

Sax mentions the alternative 19. Kh1, and concludes that
after 19. . . . Qf5 20. Qc5 Nd5 21. Nxd5 cxd5 22. f3 fxe3
23. fxe4 Qxe4 24. Bf3 Qd3 25. Qxd5 Nf4, Black retains
the advantage.

19.	...	f3!
20.	gxf3	Qh3
21.	Nxe4	...

Defense is hopeless:

(A) If 21. Qg5, then 21. . . . exf3 22. Bd3 Ng4, threatening mate at g2 and h2.

(B) If 21. fxe4, then 21. . . . Ng4 22. Bxg4 Qxg4+ 23.
Kh1 Nh4, threatening mate at g2 (and if 24. Rg1, then
24. . . . Qf3+ 25. Rg2 Qxg2#).

21.	...	Ng4!

White resigns (0-1).

Power Mate 4

Q4: Can you demonstrate that Black mates in all the lines
that count?

*P*OWER GAME *5*

Ivacic vs. Sermek
Portoroz, 1994

White starts the attack on the kingside, but weakness ensues. Black counters in the center, castling queenside and exerting pressure along the d-file. Material is sacrificed to clear the air, and Black's queen invades to the seventh rank, where White's king meets its doomsday.

English Opening A36

1.	c4	c5
2.	g3	g6
3.	Bg2	Bg7
4.	Nc3	Nc6
5.	e3	Nh6
6.	h4	. . .

After White's 6th move

These explorations on the flanks are permissible in the English, provided White doesn't lose control of the center.

| 6. | ... | d6 |
| 7. | h5 | Bg4 |

Black tries to induce weaknesses in White's pawn structure, and White goes along with it.

| 8. | f3 | Be6 |
| 9. | d3 | d5 |

The best way to blunt a kingside demonstration is a strike in the center. Here, White is unprepared for this counteroffensive.

10.	hxg6	hxg6
11.	cxd5	Bxd5
12.	Nge2	Ne5

It's doubtful that White has accomplished anything on the kingside, but Black is gaining space in the middle. With his next two moves, White tries to recover lost ground.

13.	e4	Bc6
14.	d4	cxd4
15.	Nxd4	...

After White's 15th move

| 15. | ... | Qb6 |

The overly clever combination 15. . . . Qxd4? 16. Qxd4 Nxf3+ fails in the end because the h6-knight hangs.

| 16. | Nce2 | ... |

White's pieces are going in the wrong direction. Better is the forward-moving 16. Nxc6 Qxc6 17. Qd5.

| 16. | ... | 0-0-0 |

Black uses castling not so much for defense but as a weapon of destruction. The d-file is now his.

| 17. | Kf1 | Nxf3! |
| 18. | Bxf3 | e5 |

The pin on the d-file reaps a harvest. The situation has become critical.

| 19. | Bg5 | exd4 |
| 20. | Bxd8 | Rxd8 |

After Black's 20th move

| 21. | Qb3 | d3 |

White has won the exchange and naturally wants to trade pieces. If 22. Qxb6, then 22. . . . dxe2+ picks up a fallen fruit with check.

22.	Nc3	Qe3
23.	Kg2	Qd2+
24.	Kg1	. . .

Tripping over mate in two moves (0-1). But the alternatives are not attractive either. If 24. Kf1, then 24. . . . Nf5!; or if 24. Kh3, then 24. . . . Rh8.

Power Mate 5

Q5: What routine mate did Black gather in?

*P*OWER GAME *6*

Rodriguez vs. Rakic
Vrnjacka Banja, 1977

Black proceeds too steadily and his king is trapped in the center after White seizes the a3-f8 diagonal. The attacker charges ahead in the center, the defender impairing his own chances with a weakening pawn move. White sacrifices to open lines and checks his way to a powerful pin, converting to a dynamic queen-and-rook duo. Batman and Robin get their man.

Modern Defense A42

1.	e4	g6
2.	d4	Bg7
3.	c4	d6
4.	Nc3	Nd7
5.	Nf3	e5
6.	Be2	Nh6

After Black's 6th move

Black could transpose into a King's Indian by 6. . . . Ngf6, an opening considered slightly more reliable. With the text, Black wants to continue f7-f6 and Nh6-f7, bringing his knight back to civilization.

| | 7. | h4!? | ... |

A move with a good reputation. It thwarts Black's plan, since 7. . . . f6 can be countered by 8. Bxh6 Bxh6 9. h5. To keep the h-file closed, Black would then have to play the ugly g6-g5, weakening the light squares.

	7.	...	exd4
	8.	Nxd4	Nc5
	9.	h5	c6
	10.	Bf4	Qe7?

Better would be 10. . . . Qf6!, when 11. Be3 Qe7 takes pressure off d6.

| | 11. | Bf3 | ... |

Intending 12. Nde2, unveiling a threat to the d6-pawn from the queen.

| | 11. | ... | g5? |

This doesn't help. It only strengthens White's resolve.

After Black's 11th move

12.	Nxc6!	bxc6

Or 12. . . . Qd7 13. Bxd6 Qxc6 14. e5, followed by 15. Nd5, and Black's position is in need of remedy.

13.	Bxd6	Qb7
14.	Bxc5	Qxb2

After Black's 14th move

On 14. . . . g4, White has 15. Bd4 and implicit superiority.

15.	0-0!	Qxc3

If 15. . . . Bxc3?, then 16. Qd6, threatening mate at e7. Black is walking a tightrope.

16.	e5!	...

But not 16. Qd6? because of 16. . . . Qf6, when 17. Qxf6 Bxf6 18. e5 Be7! 19. Bxc6+ Bd7 saves the day.

16.	...	Bd7

The only practical move, but practical doesn't make perfect.

17.	Bxc6!	Rd8

If 17. . . . Bxc6, then 18. Qd6, overseeing e7 and c6; and if 17. . . . 0-0-0, then 18. Qa4, aiming to damage. Without pawn cover, Black's king is woeful.

	18.	Qd6	Bf8

Black could try 18. . . . Nf5, but that loses to 19. Bxd7+ Rxd7 20. Qb8+.

	19.	Bxd7+	Rxd7
	20.	Qb8+	Rd8
	21.	Qb5+	Rd7

The rook is now pinned, and White wastes no time piling on.

	22.	Rad1	Bxc5
	23.	Qxd7+	Kf8

White now played his 24th move and Black resigned (**1-0**).

Power Mate 6

Q6: How does White satisfy the fans with fulfilling mate?

POWER GAME **7**

Gurgenidze vs. Kapengut
USSR, 1975

Black plays risky pool, accepting doubled pawns and wasting time. He further lets his forces be split in half by a piercing d-pawn pincer. White offers two rooks, which Black's queen consumes, abandoning the king to White's queen, bishop, and knight. Swift and sweet is retribution.

Queen-Pawn Game A45

1.	d4	Nf6
2.	Bg5	. . .

This is called Trompowsky's Attack internationally, but Americans know it as Bill Ruth's Opening. The Camden, New Jersey, Master was playing his opening back in the early 1920s, long before Trompowsky arrived on the scene. Ruth liked its offbeat qualities and the chance to weave some tricky traps. These same attractions hold good today.

2.	. . .	c5

In recent games Black has most often played 2. . . . Ne4, and White's response is usually 3. Bf4. Ruth liked 3. h4, and this also is occasionally played.

3.	Bxf6	gxf6

Black accepts doubled pawns to build initiative and control the center. A typical trade-off: time and space for structure.

4.	d5	Qb6
5.	Qc1	f5
6.	e3	Bg7
7.	c3	e6

After Black's 7th move

8.	Nh3!	h5?!

With 8. . . . exd5, Black cedes f4 to White's knight. Here, and on subsequent moves, d7-d6 looks right.

9.	Be2	e5
10.	f4!	e4

Is Black wasting too much time and overextending himself?

11.	Na3!	. . .

Show this game to beginners with provisos, for otherwise they might be overly willing to develop their knights to the edge of the universe.

11.	. . .	Qg6?

Last chance for 11. . . . d6. Now Black never achieves it, and his queenside pieces remain bottled up.

12.	Nb5	Na6
13.	d6!	Bf8

Also in White's favor is 13. . . . Qxg2 14. Rg1 Qxh3 15. Rxg7.

14.	Qd2!	Qxg2

After Black's 14th move

15.	Qd5!!	f6

For the moment, Black declines the double rook sacrifice. After 15. . . . Qxh1+ 16. Kd2 Qxa1, White wins by 17. Qe5+ Kd8 18. Qxh8 Ke8 19. Qe5+ Kd8 20. Ng5, threatening knightly closure at f7.

16.	Qxf5!	Qxh1+

There is nothing better, so Black sucks in the rooks.

17.	Kd2	Qxa1

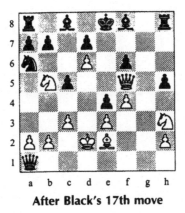

After Black's 17th move

18.	Qg6+	Kd8
19.	Qxf6+	Ke8
20.	Qe5+!	Kf7

Or 20. . . . Kd8 21. Qxh8 Qxb2+ 22. Ke1 and wins.

21.	Bc4+

Here Black resigned (1-0).

Power Mate 7

Q7: Can you illustrate forced mate in all reasonable lines?

Z. Polgar vs. NN
Budapest, 1982

White overprotects e5, assigning it strongpoint status. After occupying the e-file, White lifts her rook to the third rank and over to the g-file. At the right moment, a classic bishop sacrifice at h7 starts dismantling Black's pawn cover. The queen enters the attack, the g-file is blown with a rook sacrifice, and a cramped Black can't fend off a support mate at g7.

Queen-Pawn Game A47

1.	d4	Nf6
2.	Nf3	b6
3.	Bf4	...

This is the universal London system, which White can play against almost any black setup. The idea is to control e5, and when the square is secure, White turns to the black king.

3.	...	d5
4.	Nbd2	c5
5.	e3	e6
6.	Ne5	cxd4
7.	exd4	Be7
8.	Ndf3	0-0
9.	Bd3	Bb7
10.	0-0	Nc6
11.	c3	Rc8

After Black's 11th move

White has an ideal London: control of e5 and attacking chances against the king.

12.   h3   Nxe5

Taking on e5 doesn't bring relief. A White pawn replaces the knight, driving Black's steed from f6. With the f6-knight gone, h7 and h5 are weakened.

13.   dxe5   Ne4

The best chance, using the knight to clog up the center.

14.   Nd4   Nc5

After Black's 14th move

Black loses the thread, misplacing his pieces with one-move stabs. The knight should have stayed on e4 as long as possible.

	15.	Bc2	Ba6
	16.	Re1	Qe8

Ready to counter 17. Qh5 with 17. . . . f5. But White has no need to rush, and simply nurtures her game.

	17.	Re3	Bb7
	18.	Rg3	a6

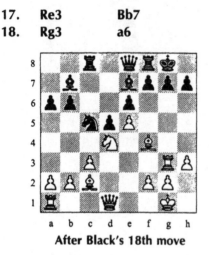

After Black's 18th move

	19.	Bxh7+!	. . .

The position explodes with this classic bishop sacrifice. White has a mating attack.

	19.	. . .	Kxh7
	20.	Qh5+	Kg8
	21.	Rxg7+	. . .

Another bombshell, obiterating the pawn cover.

	21.	. . .	Kxg7
	22.	Bh6+	Kh8
	23.	Bg5+!	. . .

Much stronger than 23. Bxf8+. Mate's the thing.

23.   . . .   Kg8

White played two more moves and Black resigned on move
25 (1-0).

Power Mate 8

Q8: How does White weave a mate?

POWER GAME 9

Kholmov vs. Zilberman
Frunze, 1989

Black forces a swap of knight for bishop, thus weakening the kingside pawn structure. White makes hay on the vulnerable squares, seeking entry along the h-file and the b1-h7 diagonal. Some tactical fireworks merely startle, until a deflective sacrifice finds a hole in the line. Queen-and-rook mate concludes.

Queen-Pawn Game A48

1.	e4	g6
2.	d4	Bg7
3.	c3	d6

Black is trying to play a Modern Defense. But with his next few moves, Kholmov manages to transpose into a Torre Attack, a line he's played for ages.

4.	Bg5	Nf6
5.	Nd2	0-0
6.	Ngf3	h6
7.	Bh4	g5
8.	Bg3	Nh5
9.	Bc4	Nxg3

After Black's 9th move

Tracking down the bishop like this is a risky operation. One can never be sure which will count more: Black's two bishops or his weakened kingside pawn structure. Here the edge appears to lie with White. He's not yet castled, so he can use the open h-file to harass Black's king.

	10.	hxg3	e6

Necessary, for White was already threatening 11. Nxg5 hxg5 12. Qh5, invading on the square weakened by the advance g6-g5.

11.	Qe2	d5
12.	Bb3	b6
13.	0-0-0	...

White's king is perfectly safe. Castling queenside enables him to throw both rooks at Black's king.

13.	...	Ba6

Harassing tactics. Black can't find a decent plan, so he attacks White's queen.

14.	Qe3	Nc6

After Black's 14th move

15.	Nh2!	...

Simple but powerful. The coming Nh2-g4 will be decisive.

15.	...	dxe4

Black tries to organize a defense. Exchanging off the e4-pawn enables him to post his knight at f5. Note that 15. . . . e5, trying to mix it up in the center, can be ignored because of 16. Ng4!, assailing h6 and recharging White's attack.

16.	Qxe4	Ne7
17.	Bc2	...

A new danger—mate on h7.

17.	...	Re8

With 17. . . . Nf5?, White scores on the b1-h7 diagonal with 18. g4.

18.	Ng4	Nf5
19.	Qf3!	...

After White's 19th move

There's nothing to be done about 20. Bxf5, dynamiting Black's shields.

19.	...	Kf8
20.	Bxf5	exf5
21.	Nxh6	Re6

After 21. . . . Be2 22. Qxf5 (threatening mate at f7) 22. . . . Bxh6 23. Rxh6 Bxd1 24. Kxd1, Black is impuissant, playing

without his queen-rook. For example, if 24. . . . Qe7 (else 25. Rh7, or 25. Nf3, and White's attack continues), then 25. Rh8+ Kg7 26. Qh7+ Kf6 27. Qh6+ Kf5 28. g4+, and mate shortly.

	22.	Nxf5	Be2

It looks like an annoying fork, but Black has missed White's surprise zwischenzug.

	23.	Nxg7!	Kxg7

The point is that 23. . . . Bxf3 is met by 24. Nxe6+ fxe6 25. Rh8+, regaining the queen by skewer. White now played his 23rd move and Black resigned (1-0).

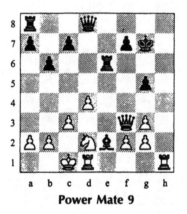

Power Mate 9

Q9: How did White crumble Black's remaining defenses with mate?

POWER GAME **10**

Alexandria vs. Schnepp
Biel, 1994

Black develops quickly, castling and positioning a rook at e8. White takes a pawn, opening the e-file, and Black offers a knight at f2 to undermine the shielding e-pawn. White's king tries to forage for itself, but is inundated by tactics (a discovery, doubled rooks, an exchange sacrifice, and a series of tortuous queen threats). It is driven outward until check after check produces mate far down the board.

Budapest Defense A52

1.	d4	Nf6
2.	c4	e5

The Budapest. Black hopes to regain his gambited pawn or obtain an equivalent value in initiative and attack.

3.	dxe5	Ng4
4.	Nf3	Bc5
5.	e3	Nc6
6.	b3	0-0
7.	Bb2	Re8
8.	Bd3	d6

To clear the central lines for bellicosity.

| 9. | exd6 | . . . |

After White's 9th move

This is asking for it, opening the e-file for Black's rook and encouraging a tactical melee.

| | 9. | ... | Nxf2!? |

A suggestion of Zeitlin and Glaskow (two analysts of repute), setting White some difficult problems. His pawn bucklers are wiped out and his king is forced into the great unknown, which isn't so great.

| | 10. | Kxf2 | Rxe3 |

Capturing to set up a nasty discovery, gaining time and accelerating the attack. Black will soon be able to double on the e-file.

| | 11. | Kf1 | Bg4 |
| | 12. | Be2 | Bxf3! |

Destroying White's hold over h4, enabling Black's queen to join the fray.

| | 13. | Bxf3 | Qh4 |

After Black's 13th move

It's clear that Black has a dangerous attack, and it's hard to offer White good advice. One try is 14. d7, guarding e8, preventing Black's a8-rook from backing up its partner at e3.

	14.	**Nd2**	**Rae8!**

This coupling of rooks imparts new vigor to the onslaught. The immediate threat is 15. . . . Re1+ 16. Qxe1 Rxe1+ 17. Rxe1 Qf2#. Faced with such browbeating, White must weaken his position further.

15.	**g3**	**Qh3 +**
16.	**Bg2**	**Qf5 +**
17.	**Bf3**	**. . .**

Or 17. Nf3 Re1+ 18. Qxe1 Qd3+ 19. Qe2 Qxe2, mate most cruel.

17.	**. . .**	**Qd3 +**
18.	**Kg2**	**. . .**

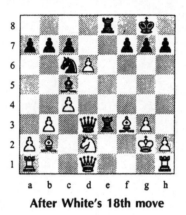

After White's 18th move

Can Black make headway?

>   18.   ...   Re2+!

This exchange sacrifice answers the question most emphatically. The end is in sight.

>   19.   Bxe2   Rxe2+
>   20.   Kh3   Qf5+!
>   21.   Kh4   ...

If 21. g4, White can still count on being mated by 21. . . . Qd3+ 22. Kh4 Bf2+, etc. After the actual reply, **21. Kh4**, White got mated in four moves **(0-1)**.

Power Mate 10

Q10: How did Black solve the mystery of this particular chess universe in four moves?

POWER GAME *11*

Hausner vs. Pribyl
Policka, 1993

White develops his pieces to instill weaknesses, and Black replies with pawn advances that overextend his own position even further. White's queen and knight encamp on the weakened squares, while his bishop scours the a2-g8 diagonal. Finally he compels the exchange of queens, unsheathing the h-file and pressing a mating force into line.

Alekhine Defense B02

1.	e4	Nf6
2.	e5	Nd5
3.	Nc3	Nxc3
4.	bxc3	d6
5.	Nf3	...

Usually White plays 5. f4 to reinforce the e5-pawn. The text is supposed to be harmless, so much so that it's practically been forgotten. Go back far enough, though, and you'll discover that Yates used 5. Nf3 to beat Colle at Hastings in 1926.

5.	...	dxe5
6.	Nxe5	Nd7
7.	Nf3	e6
8.	d4	b6?

After Black's 8th move

Uncomplicated and good is 8. . . . Be7 and 9. . . . 0-0. The text leads to problems. It delays kingside development and weakens the light queenside squares, especially c6.

9.	Bb5!	Bd6

No time for 9. . . . Bb7? because of 10. Ne5, seizing upon c6 and d7.

10.	Bg5!	f6

Black accepts the impairment of his pawn structure. If 10. . . . Be7?, then 11. Ne5 Bxg5 12. Qf3 hits a8 and f7 simultaneously. Here we see how one weakness (c6) can engender another (e6).

11.	Bd2	Bb7
12.	Qe2	Qe7
13.	0-0	a6

If 13. . . . 0-0, Black must contend with a2-a4, along with Bb5-a6. The text is designed to dispel the b5-bishop so that Black can advance his backward e6-pawn.

14.	Bd3	e5?!

After Black's 14th move

The e-pawn has moved forward, but that's not the end of the story. At e5, it's still subject to attack. And there is a new weakness at f5.

15.	Rae1	0-0
16.	Nh4	Qf7

Or 16. . . . g6 (weakening h6), inviting 17. Bh6 Rfe8 18. Qg4.

17.	Qg4	e4

If 17. . . . Bd5 (apparently strengthening the a2-g8 diagonal), then 18. c4 Be6 (18. . . . Bxc4 19. Nf5) 19. Qe2 Qe7 20. f4! calls out White's dominance.

18.	Nf5!	. . .

The exchange 18. Bxe4 releases the pressure: 18. . . . Bxe4 19. Qxe4 (19. Rxe4?? f5—a fork) 19. . . . Qxa2. But now the black e-pawn is ready for seizure.

18.	. . .	Qg6

After Black's 18th move

| 19. | Bc4+! | ... |

Stronger than 19. Qxg6 hxg6 20. Nxd6 cxd6 21. Bxe4. The weakness of the e-pawn has led to a more serious weakness: the fragility of the king along the a2-g8 diagonal.

| 19. | ... | Kh8 |
| 20. | Qxg6! | hxg6 |

White played his 21st move and Black resigned (**1-0**).

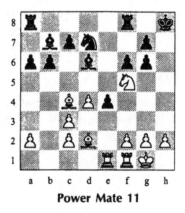

Power Mate 11

Q11: What maneuver allowed White to configure a mating net?

*P*OWER GAME *12*

Nigmadzianov vs. Kaplin
USSR, 1977

Instead of routinely taking back on e2, White creates tension with a potent in-between move, sacrificing a piece and messing up Black at e6. Black's development is further jammed by another constricting pawn move. With unerring precision, White invades Black's fortress, gives discovered check, and sacrifices his queen to devise smothered mate.

Alekhine Defense B05

1.	e4	Nf6
2.	e5	Nd5
3.	d4	d6
4.	Nf3	Bg4
5.	Be2	c6

After Black's 5th move

When players get tired of 5. . . . e6, they usually turn to 5. . . . c6, Salo Flohr's variation from the 1930s. Black secures the long a8-h1 diagonal and prepares Bg4xf3, followed by d6xe5.

| 6. | c4 | ... |

Usual is 6. 0-0 or 6. Ng5. The text derives from Levenfish (a noted scholar and player). The concept is to use Nbd2 in order to recapture on f3 with the d2-knight, replacing one knight with another. But if White plays 6. Nbd2 he blocks the c1-bishop, allowing 6. . . . Nf4.

| 6. | ... | Nb6 |
| 7. | Nbd2 | N8d7 |

If 7. . . . dxe5, then 8. Nxe5 Bxe2 9. Qxe2 Qxd4 10. Ndf3, and Black must waste time moving his queen as White's forces nucleate for aggression.

| 8. | Ng5! | Bxe2 |

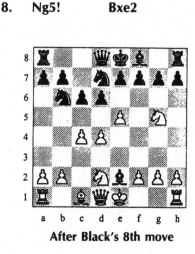

After Black's 8th move

| 9. | e6! | f6 |

A timely zwischenzug. If 9. . . . Bxd1??, gaining the queen, then 10. exf7#, obtaining the king.

| 10. | Qxe2 | fxg5 |
| 11. | Ne4! | ... |

The position is level after 11. exd7+ Qxd7 12. Ne4 0-0-0. White's piece sacrifice is far from clear, but over the board the defender's task is not so easy.

| 11. | ... | Nf6 |
| 12. | Nxg5 | Qc7 |

In Vogt-Roguli, Balatonbereny, 1986, Black decided to return the piece immediately by 12. . . . Nxc4, with the game ending in a draw after 27 moves. But that's not this game.

| 13. | Nf7 | Rg8 |
| 14. | g4! | h6 |

Weakening g6, which in turn weakens h5.

| 15. | h4 | d5 |

Black could reduce the pressure on his game by giving back some material with 15. . . . g5 16. hxg5 hxg5 17. Bxg5 Rxg5, but 18. Nxg5 0-0-0 19. Nf7 Re8 20. g5 sustains the initiative.

| 16. | c5 | Nc8? |

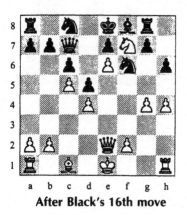

After Black's 16th move

An improvement seems to be 16. . . . Nc4. Now Black remains greatly constricted, unable to complete harmonious development.

17.	g5	Ne4
18.	gxh6	gxh6
19.	Qh5	...

Invading on the indefensible square. A discovered check is envisioned.

19.   ...   Nf6

This assails White's queen, but it doesn't cope with the full magnitude of the threat, and Black was forced to resign after two more moves (1-0).

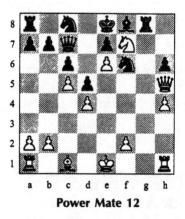

Power Mate 12

Q12: How does White make horsemeat of Black in three moves?

POWER GAME *13*

Tal vs. Tringov
Amsterdam, 1964

White offers a poisoned pawn for development, and Black must spend time disengaging his queen. After a line-opening central exchange, White sinks his queen into a soft spot at d6, backing it with a rook. Black blocks the d-file to stop the fleecing, but the c4-bishop is sacrificed at f7, the enemy king is drawn out, and White's queen and knight seize the game for mate.

Modern Defense B06

1.	e4	g6
2.	d4	Bg7
3.	Nc3	d6
4.	Nf3	c6
5.	Bg5	Qb6?!

Safe and sane is 5. . . . Nf6, with transposition to a Pirc Defense. Tringov means to snatch the b2-pawn. The only person who took b2-pawns and lived to tell the tale was Bobby Fischer, and that was in his favorite Najdorf Sicilian, and that was years ago.

6.	Qd2	Qxb2
7.	Rb1	Qa3
8.	Bc4	Qa5
9.	0-0	e6

After Black's 9th move

White has completed development and is ready to start the middlegame. Black is still in the early stages of the opening, with his pieces undeveloped and lacking potential. Advantage: White.

	10.	**Rfe1**	**a6**

Black has trouble just bringing out his pieces. For example, 10. . . . Ne7 runs into 11. Bxe7 Kxe7 12. Nd5+ and 13. Qxa5 (bye-bye, Queenie). And 10. . . . Nd7 fails against 11. Nb5!, again exploiting the poor placement of Black's queen. Tringov's a7-a6 is designed to prepare 11. . . . Nd7, when 12. Nb5 loses to 12. . . . axb5, and the a8-rook protects the queen.

	11.	**Bf4!**	**. . .**

White is ready to start all-out warfare and switches focus to the weak d6-pawn.

	11.	**. . .**	**e5?**

This is refuted beautifully. Better would be retreating the queen to d8.

	12.	**dxe5**	**dxe5**

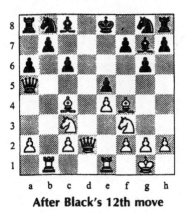

After Black's 12th move

13. Qd6! ...

Offering Black a choice of pieces to take. At that time, he
was partial to the c3-knight.

13. ... Qxc3

If 13. . . . exf4, then 14. Nd5! Two continuations Black
might have tried were:

(A) 14. . . . cxd5 15. exd5+ Be6 16. dxe6 f6 17. Rxb7,
with 18. Rxb8+ or 18. Rxg7 to follow. or

(B) Declining the knight with 14. . . . Nd7, when 15.
Ng5 Be5 16. Nc7+ Qxc7 17. Bxf7+ Kd8 is mated by 18.
Ne6#.

The only move to prolong the game is 13. . . . Bf8,
pointed out by Cafferty. But after 14. Qxe5+ Qxe5 15.
Bxe5, Black has a horrible position.

14. Red1 ...

Threatening mate. The idea is to force Black to turn over
control of e6 by forcing Nb8-d7, blocking out the c8-bishop.

14. ... Nd7

After Black's 14th move

This fails, but does 14. . . . Qa5 (or 14. . . . Bd7) achieve more? After 15. Rxb7 (a deflecting rook sacrifice) Bxb7 16. Bxf7+ Kxf7 17. Ng5+, Black is ill.

15.   Bxf7+   Kxf7

It's crunch time after 15. . . . Kd8 16. Bg5+. White now played a two-shot and Black resigned on the 17th move (**1-0**).

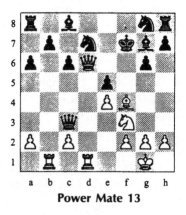

Power Mate 13

Q13: Can you provide the details of Tal's aesthetic conclusion?

POWER GAME *14*

Yeo vs. Erdal-Smith
London, 1979

After advancing the e-pawn to gain space, White force-feeds Black the f-pawn and sacrifices two knights to get at Black's gut. A devastating discovery is set up on the central files, which Black shuns, only to be eviscerated by sharpened bishops. However you cut it, it's mate.

Modern Defense B06

1.	e4	g6
2.	d4	Bg7
3.	Nc3	d6
4.	f4	a6

The most often played move here is 4. . . . c6. Another way to go is to transpose to a Pirc Defense with 4. . . . Nf6.

5.	Nf3	b5
6.	Bd3	Bb7
7.	0-0	Nd7
8.	e5	. . .

After White's 8th move

While Black has been creeping around the perimeter, White has been expanding outward, here striking in the center.

8.	...	b4
9.	Ne4	d5
10.	Neg5	e6

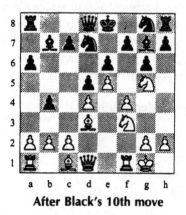

After Black's 10th move

Black tries to keep the position closed, but it can't be done. White has too many detonating devices.

| 11. | f5! | gxf5 |

If 11. . . . exf5, then 12. e6 perforates.

12.	Nxf7!	Kxf7
13.	Ng5 +	Ke7
14.	Nxe6!	Kxe6

You've heard of the double bishop sacrifice? This is the double knight sacrifice.

| 15. | Bxf5 + | Ke7 |
| 16. | Bg5 + | ... |

After White's 16th move

The position reminds one of the second game of the Morphy-Meek match, New York, 1857. Remember that?

	16.	...	Ndf6

Or 16. . . . Bf6 17. exf6+ Ndxf6 18. Qe1+ Kf7 19. Be6+ Kg6 20. Qg3 Ne4 21. Bf7+ Kg7 22. Bf6+ Kxf7 23. Qg7+, winning quickly.

	17.	Qe1!	Kf7
	18.	Be6+!!	...

Trying to lure the king to the discoverable e-file. If 18. . . . Kxe6, then 19. exf6+ and 20. fxg7.

	18.	...	Kg6
	19.	Qg3	Ne4

This fails to White's next move (1-0).

Power Mate 14

Q14: What should White do?

POWER GAME *15*

Gustone vs. Bluma
USSR, 1979

Castled on the opposite side, White advances the h-pawn to open lines against the enemy king. Black's situation has been jeopardized by recapturing away from the center. White's bishop swiftly annexes the uncovered a2-g8 diagonal, and though Black's queen keeps the door to the h-file closed, a deflective rook sacrifice detaches the hinges.

Pirc Defense B08

1.	e4	d6
2.	d4	g6
3.	Nf3	Bg7
4.	Nc3	Nf6
5.	Be2	0-0
6.	h3	Nbd7
7.	Be3	c6
8.	Qd2	e5
9.	dxe5	dxe5
10.	0-0-0	Qe7

After Black's 10th move

This is a rare sideline of the Pirc. White's next move is a speculative conception. He's willing to allow the trade of his dark-square bishop in order to open the h-file.

11.	h4	Ng4
12.	h5	Nxe3
13.	Qxe3	Nf6

Black amasses his forces around his castled king, but fully playable was 13. . . . Qc5, trying to reduce the ferocity of the oncoming clash by trading queens.

| 14. | hxg6 | fxg6 |

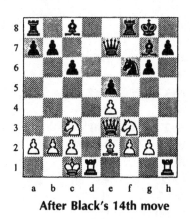

After Black's 14th move

Much safer would be 14. . . . hxg6, keeping the a2-g8 diagonal closed. Black was concerned with White's h-file activity and wanted to maintain some plating there, but taking away from the center (fxg6) is still worse.

| 15. | Bc4+ | Kh8? |

Black rejected 15. . . . Be6 because of 16. Nxe5, but he should have continued analyzing the line further: 16. . . . Bxc4 17. Nxc4 Ng4 18. Qh3 h5 gives good chances to defend.

| 16. | Nh4 | ... |

Threatening 17. Nxg6+, thus forcing Black's queen to retreat.

| 16. | ... | Qe8 |
| 17. | Qg5 | ... |

Again, the threat is 18. Nxg6, so Black tries to block the h-file.

| 17. | ... | Nh5 |

After Black's 17th move

| 18. | Rd8! | Qxd8 |

Now it's time. With his opponent's queen out of position, White was able to force resignation on move 20 (1-0).

Power Mate 15

Q15: Can you find White's good-as-gold mate?

POWER GAME *16*

Stangl vs. Azmaiparashvili
Tilburg, 1994

White spearheads the assault by pushing the e-pawn. Swinging to the queenside, he nags Black along the a4-e8 diagonal, though defense seems possible. But then a sudden rook lift to d3 quickens the c-file, and White's queen and rook ride the freeway to a back-rank mate.

Pirc Defense B08

1.	d4	d6
2.	Nf3	g6
3.	e4	Bg7
4.	Nc3	Nf6
5.	Bf4	. . .

This practically forgotten line packs a punch if Black is not careful.

5.	. . .	c6

The recommended book moves are 5. . . . c5 and 5. . . . Nc6, but the text is also good if followed up properly.

6.	Qd2	Qa5
7.	h3	Nbd7
8.	0-0-0	b5?

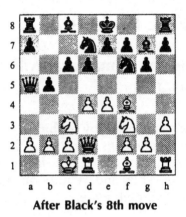

After Black's 8th move

But this is a mistake. Black should have tried 8. . . . 0-0, getting his king to safety.

9.	e5!	b4
10.	exf6	bxc3
11.	Qxc3!	. . .

In Korchnoi-Pirc, USSR vs. Yugoslavia, 1957 (remember it?), White played the imaginative 11. fxg7 cxd2+ 12. Bxd2 Qxd2+ 13. Rxd2 and won a long, difficult endgame. The text is convincing.

11.	. . .	Qf5

After Black's 11th move

After 11. . . . Qxc3, Black loses on the spot to 12. fxg7!

12.	fxg7	Qxf4 +
13.	Kb1	Rg8
14.	Qxc6	Rb8
15.	Bb5	. . .

Threatens an inroad by 16. Qc7; if 16. . . . Rxb5?, then 17. Qxc8#; and if 15. . . . d5?, then 16. Ne5.

15.	. . .	Kd8

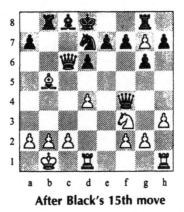

After Black's 15th move

16.	Rd3!	. . .

Effortless chess. The threat of 17. Rc3 is decisive if followed by 18. Qc7 + .

16.	. . .	Qf5

If 16. . . . d5, then 17. Ne5 Nxe5 18. dxe5 Be6 19. Rxd5 + is brutal.

17.	Rc3	Qxb5

This loses at once. White played his 18th move and Black gave up (1-0).

Power Mate 16

Q16: How does White mate the hapless black king?

POWER GAME **17**

Stein vs. Liberson
Erevan, 1965

Positive energy is employed to build White's development, which empowers the headlong opening of the h-file. Unexpected shifts of queen and knight fuel the aggression, but it takes a trade to expose Black's back rank to invasion. A queen sacrifice unplugs the juice, and Black is mated.

Pirc Defense B09

1.	e4	d6
2.	d4	Nf6
3.	Nc3	g6
4.	f4	Bg7
5.	Nf3	0-0
6.	e5	. . .

Fashionable at the time. Today 6. Bd3 and 6. Be3 are in vogue.

6.	. . .	Nfd7

Despite the reduced force, White would be left with a small but sure edge in the endgame after 6. . . . dxe5 7. dxe5 Qxd1+ 8. Kxd1.

7.	h4	. . .

Preparing an assault on the black king by hoping to blow out the h-file. Meanwhile, as strategy dictates, Black will counterattack in the center.

7.	. . .	c5
8.	h5	cxd4
9.	Qxd4	. . .

The piece sacrifice 9. hxg6 dxc3 is in Black's favor.

| 9. | ... | dxe5 |
| 10. | Qf2 | ... |

If 10. fxe5?, then 10. . . . Nxe5 gains the e-pawn. With this attacking retreat, White envisages a kingside offensive with Qf2-h4.

| 10. | ... | e6?! |

For a short time this was the recommended move for Black, stopping queen to h4. But then, a year later, 10. . . . e4! was introduced (Padevsky-Matanovic, Havana Olympiad, 1966), and the world hasn't been the same since.

| 11. | hxg6 | fxg6 |
| 12. | Qg3 | ... |

After White's 12th move

12.	...	exf4
13.	Bxf4	Qa5
14.	Bd2	Nf6
15.	Bc4	Nc6
16.	0-0-0	Qc5

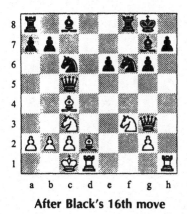

After Black's 16th move

White's pawn gift can now be seen largely as a gambit for development. All his pieces are in the game, while Black's queen-bishop and queen-rook are still on their starting squares, unable to get out of the block.

	17.	**Qh4**	. . .

Guards the c4-bishop while taking aim at h7, ideally merging defense with attack.

	17.	. . .	**Nh5**

There's still no time to develop the queenside: 17. . . . Bd7? collides with 18. Ne4! Nxe4 19. Qxh7+ Kf7 20. Bh6, along with Rd1xd7+ and virtual mayhem.

	18.	**Ne4!**	**Qb6**

If 18. . . . Qxc4?, 19. Nf6+ wins the queen by discovery, h4 to c4.

	19.	**c3**	**Na5**

Pushes the bishop back, but reduces coverage at d8.

	20.	**Be2**	**h6**
	21.	**g4**	**Nf4**

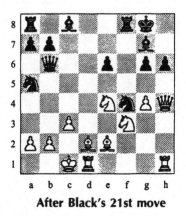

After Black's 21st move

22.	Bxf4	Rxf4
23.	Rd8+	Rf8

Other moves don't ward off the inevitable:

(A) 23. . . . Kh7 24. Nfg5#.

(B) 23. . . . Kf7 24. Nd6+, forcing Black to surrender his queen to stave off mate.

(C) 23. . . . Bf8 24. Nf6+ Kg7 (or 24. . . . Kf7 25. Ne5+ Ke7 26. Nd5# or Ng8#) 25. Qxh6+ Kxf6 26. Qxf8#.

24.	Nf6+!	Kh8

On 24. . . . Bxf6, there follows 25. Rxf8+ Kxf8 26. Qxf6+, winning. Here, White played his 25th move and Black resigned (1-0).

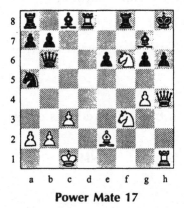

Power Mate 17

Q17: How did Stein conclude this little masterpiece?

*P*OWER GAME *18*

Prie vs. Sarno
Debrecen, 1992

White advances his center pawns to usurp space. His anchored pawn at e6 impairs Black's coordination. Though Black eventually wins the pawn, it's at great cost. White's pieces move in. By the time Black clears his home rank, he is needy for kingside reserves and White's rook has assumed the seventh. A vaporizing rook sacrifice clears the h-file, letting White's queen and bishop render a criss-cross mate.

Pirc Defense B09

1.	e4	d6
2.	d4	Nf6
3.	Nc3	g6
4.	f4	Bg7
5.	Nf3	0-0
6.	Bd3	Na6
7.	0-0	c5
8.	d5	Rb8

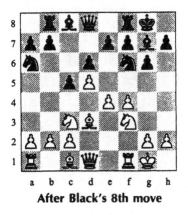

After Black's 8th move

More typical over the years has been 8. . . . Bg4.

>   **9.   e5!?   ...**

Introduced by Dolmatov in his fascinating game with Pfleger, Bundesliga, 1991. For several years it put 8. . . . Rb8 out of commission.

>   **9.   ...   Nd7?**

Pfleger's move 9. . . . dxe5 also leaves Black in trouble. Best is 9. . . . Ne8!, when e6 is still guarded by the c8-bishop.

>   **10.   e6   fxe6**
>   **11.   dxe6   Nb6**

Black can keep his knight on the kingside with 11. . . . Nf6, but then White's bishop gets the c4-square. The pawn at e6 severely screws up Black's harmony and peace of mind.

>   **12.   Ng5   ...**

With ideas of 13. f5, as well as 13. Nxh7 Kxh7 14. Qh5 +, and who knows where that will lead?

>   **12.   ...   c4**
>   **13.   Be2   Nc5**
>   **14.   Bg4   Rf6**

After Black's 14th move

Black has managed to surround the e6-pawn, but now White extracts his price.

15.	Be3	Nxe6
16.	Nd5!	Nxg5

Not 16. . . . Nxd5 17. Qxd5, pinning and winning the knight at e6.

17.	Bxb6	axb6
18.	Nxf6 +	Bxf6
19.	fxg5	Bxb2
20.	Rb1	Be5

After Black's 20th move

Black has two pawns for the exchange, but White's next few moves reestablish the blockade at e6, and Black can hardly budge.

21.	Qd5 +	Kh8
22.	Be6	Bd7
23.	Rf7	Bc6

Shooing away the rook with 23. . . . Be8 runs afoul: 24. Rf8 + Kg7 25. Rg8#. A rook and bishop together can do it all.

24.	Qxc4	b5?

Hastens the finale, but with Rb1-f1 looming, the end was near anyway. White played his 25th move and Black abandoned all hope (1-0).

Power Mate 18

Q18: How did White lure the black king into Dante's Inferno for a criss-cross mate?

*P*OWER GAME *19*

Kosten vs. Mailfert
Italy, 1993

White accepts an isolated queen-pawn and proceeds to develop logically. His rooks grab key files and his bishops and knights deploy supportively. Black blockades the d-pawn, but White's knight takes an imperious stand on e5. Black jumps to recapture on d5 with his knight, abandoning h5 to White's queen. A classic bishop sacrifice ensues, followed by a rook lift, and the roof is razed.

Caro-Kann Defense B10

1.	c4	c6
2.	e4	d5
3.	cxd5	cxd5
4.	exd5	Qxd5

Another way to go is 4. . . . Nf6, delaying the recapture of the d5-pawn until it can be done with a knight.

5.	Nc3	Qd6
6.	d4	Nf6
7.	Bc4	e6
8.	Nf3	Be7
9.	0-0	0-0
10.	Qe2	Nc6

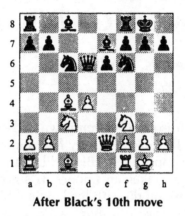

After Black's 10th move

A typical isolated queen-pawn position. In the following series of moves, each side tries to complete development while
strengthening and occupying their central strongpoints: e5
for White and d5 for Black.

11.	Rd1	Nb4

A standard maneuver. Black repositions his knight to occupy
d5, blockading the isolated pawn.

12.	Bg5	Nbd5
13.	Ne5	...

And now White's knight edges near the precipice, with a
vast overlook of Black's encampment.

13.	...	a6
14.	Rac1	...

White's rooks are placed excellently on crucial files, with
agreeable piece play emanating from White's power base:
the isolated d-pawn.

14.	...	Rd8
15.	Bd3	Bd7
16.	Nxd5	Nxd5?

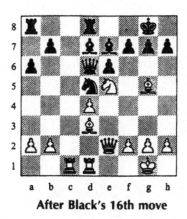

After Black's 16th move

The correct recapture would be 16. . . . exd5. From d5 the knight is unable to fulfill kingside obligations, leaving both h7 and h5 vulnerable.

17.	Bxh7+!	Kxh7
18.	Qh5+	Kg8
19.	Qxf7+	Kh7

After Black's 19th move

20.	Rd3	. . .

A standard rook lift to the third rank, threatening mate at h3. Black tries to cover with his lone kingside defender, but it's not enough.

20.	...	Bxg5
21.	Rh3 +	Bh6

White now crashed through with a bold 22nd move and Black resigned (1-0).

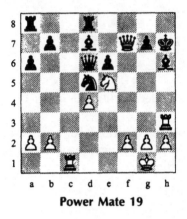

Power Mate 19

Q19: Is there a mate in two?

*P*OWER GAME *20*

Khalifman vs. Seirawan
Wijk ann Zee, 1991

It begins with a space edge, in the clarion call of a protected passed pawn. The plot thickens when White aims a bishop at the kingside. A trade lets the knight have the f5 spotlight until the queen enters to rave reviews. A knight sacrifice finally breaks up the house, as the curtain closes on mate.

Caro-Kann Defense B15

1.	e4	c6
2.	d4	d5
3.	Nc3	dxe4
4.	Nxe4	Nf6
5.	Nxf6 +	exf6
6.	c3	Bd6
7.	Bd3	0-0
8.	Ne2	Re8

After Black's 8th move

| 9. | 0-0 | . . . |

A relatively new idea. The standard treatment is 9. Qc2, with the motive of castling queenside.

| 9. | . . . | Qc7 |

Khalifman suggests leaving the queen at home and concentrating on developing the minor pieces by either 9. . . . Bg4 or 9. . . . Nd7.

| 10. | Ng3 | Be6 |
| 11. | f4! | c5 |

Black is in poor shape after 11. . . . Nd7 12. f5, as in Zapata-Hodgson, Palma de Mallorca, 1989, but the text is not much of an improvement.

| 12. | d5! | Bd7 |

White stands well after 12. . . . Bxd5 13. Qh5, but a better practical choice might have been 12. . . . c4.

| 13. | c4 | Na6 |

After Black's 13th move

White has a solidly protected passed d-pawn and this gives him a clear advantage. Black's plan, starting with Nb8-a6, is to blockade the d-pawn by bringing his knight to d6. The knight maneuver takes considerable time, as the squares c7, e8, and d6 must all be vacated.

14.	**Qf3**	**Qb6**
15.	**b3**	**Bf8**
16.	**Bb2**	**Nc7**
17.	**Bf5!**	**Bxf5**
18.	**Nxf5**	**Red8**
19.	**Rae1**	**Ne8**
20.	**Qh5**	**Qa5**

After Black's 20th move

It's clear that the intended 20. . . . Nd6 fails to 21. Nh6+ gxh6 22. Qg4+ Bg7 23. Bxf6 Nf5 24. Bxd8.

21.	**Rxe8!**	**Rxe8**
22.	**Nh6+**	**gxh6**

Declining the knight increases the opportunity for a smothered mate, as in 22. . . . Kh8 23. Qxf7 Be7 24. Qg8+ Rxg8 25. Nf7#. White played his 23rd move and Black resigned (**1-0**).

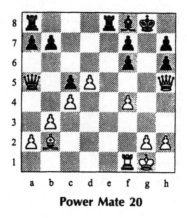

Power Mate 20

Q20: Can you show a forced mate?

POWER GAME 21

Browne vs. Bellon
Las Palmas, 1977

One bishop-pawn is advanced to c5 to gain space, the other to f5 to foster attack. When Black takes the latter pawn, White pitches the exchange to imperil the enemy king. A nuclear force gathers on the kingside until surrender terms are offered by queen sacrifice. Forcing checks behead the king.

Caro-Kann Defense B16

1.	e4	c6
2.	d4	d5
3.	Nd2	dxe4
4.	Nxe4	Nf6

In the 1990s this has been replaced by 4. . . . Nbd7, preparing the recapture on f6 with a piece instead of a pawn.

5.	Nxf6	gxf6
6.	Be2	. . .

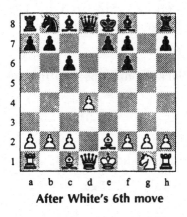

After White's 6th move

Lasker's move, avoiding the pin: 6. Nf3 Bg4.

6.	...	Bf5
7.	Nf3	Qc7
8.	0-0	e6
9.	c4	Nd7
10.	Be3	Bd6?!

After Black's 10th move

Castling queenside, 10. . . . 0-0-0, would be preferable. The text walks into Browne's novelty.

11.	c5!	Be7

If 11. . . . Bf4, then 12. Qd2 Bxe3 13. Qxe3, followed by Nf3-d2-c4-d6, a Browne-ian movement.

12.	Nd2	...

This prevents Black from consolidating with Bf5-e4 and Be4-d5.

12.	...	0-0?
13.	f4!	...

Preparing to trap the bishop with 14. g4 and 15. f5.

13.	...	Bg6

After Black's 13th move

14.	f5!	Bxf5
15.	Rxf5	exf5
16.	Bd3	Rfe8

The desperate 16. . . . f4?? is a failure after 17. Qg4+ Kh8 18. Qf5, with the idea of Qf5xh7#. The world is dominated by ideas.

17.	Bxf5	Nf8
18.	Ne4!	Kh8
19.	Qh5	Ng6
20.	Rf1	Rg8
21.	Rf3	Qa5?

The only way to hang on was 21. . . . Rg7 22. Bh6 Rag8. But not 22. . . . Rgg8, because of 23. Rh3 Rad8 24. Bf8! Nxf8 25. Qxh7+ Nxh7 26. Rxh7#. White now played a cogent 22nd move and forced Black's retirement from the battlefield **(1-0)**.

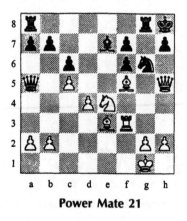

Power Mate 21

Q21: What is White's forced mate in five?

POWER GAME **22**

Karpov vs. Hort
Bugojno, 1978

Trading knight for bishop on g6, White saddles his opponent
with weak pawns. A siege pummels Black where it hurts,
and White cedes rook for knight to make way for an invasion.
With the center as his power base, White's queen and cross-
firing bishops undo Black's defensive armor. Mate is forged
with variegated tactical steel.

Caro-Kann Defense B17

1.	e4	c6
2.	d4	d5
3.	Nd2	dxe4
4.	Nxe4	Nd7
5.	Nf3	Ngf6
6.	Nxf6 +	Nxf6
7.	Ne5	. . .

White immediately moves into the strong square e5. From
there, the knight oversees just about everything.

7.	. . .	Bf5?

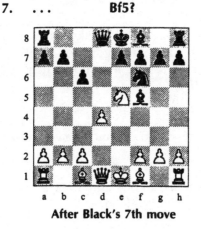

After Black's 7th move

Today this has been replaced by 7. . . . Be6 or 7. . . . Nd7.

8.	c3	e6
9.	g4	Bg6
10.	h4	h5

The game Karpov-Zaitsev, Kuibyshev, 1970, went: 10. . . . Bd6 11. Qe2! c5 12. Bg2!, which preserved White's advantage. Meanwhile, 10. . . . Be4 loses to 11. f3 Bd5 12. c4. Hort's move was likely meant to be an improvement, but he overlooked something.

11.	g5	Nd5
12.	Nxg6	fxg6

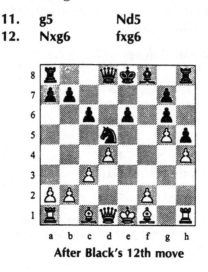

After Black's 12th move

Black's position looks a bit shaky after this weakness-inducing exchange, but he might get by if he slithers his knight to f5. Karpov's next five moves deal with offsetting this very possibility.

	13.	Qc2!	. . .

Focusing on the g6-weakness and drawing out Black's king.

	13.	. . .	Kf7

If 13. . . . Ne7, then 14. Bc4 and 15. Qe4, so Black makes the concession of moving his king.

14.	Rh3!	Ne7
15.	Bc4!	Nf5
16.	Rf3!	Qd7
17.	Rxf5 +!	gxf5
18.	Qxf5 +	Ke7
19.	Qe4	Re8

After Black's 19th move

Black can hardly move. In the next phase, White simply completes his development and targets the weak e6-pawn.

20.	Bf4	Kd8
21.	Qe5	...

To stop the bishop from moving to d6.

21.	...	Rg8
22.	0-0-0	g6
23.	Re1	Bg7

The bishop is finally out, but it's too late.

24.	Qb8 +	Ke7

Or 24. . . . Qc8 25. Qxa7.

25.	Rxe6 +!

Black resigns **(1-0)**.

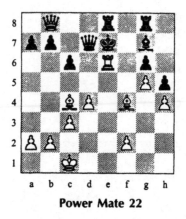

Power Mate 22

Q22: Can you find all the mates?

POWER GAME *23*

Chandler vs. Jacoby
Hamburg, 1980

Though pieces are traded, White maintains initiative by menacing the enemy queen. Also Black's king must stay in the center, exposed to the elements. Heralding the end, White's intrusive rook cuts off retreat, while major piece commandos storm Black's battlements and swat the king.

Sicilian Defense B22

1.	e4	c5
2.	c3	d5
3.	exd5	Qxd5
4.	d4	Nc6

In recent years, theory has preferred 4. . . . Nf6.

5.	Nf3	Bg4
6.	Be2	cxd4

Otherwise, White plays c3-c4 and d4-d5, with a big space edge. Now White gets c3 for the queen-knight.

7.	cxd4	e6

Not 7. . . . Bxf3 8. Bxf3 Qxd4??, because of 9. Bxc6+ and 10. Qxd4, winning Black's queen.

8.	Nc3	Qd7

The "book" choices are 8. . . . Bb4, 8. . . . Qd8, 8. . . . Qd6, and 8. . . . Qa5, the last being the most reliable.

9.	0-0	Nf6
10.	h3	Bh5

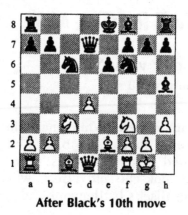

After Black's 10th move

The position is in White's favor after 10. . . . Bxf3 11. Bxf3 Nxd4 12. Bxb7.

| 11. | Ne5! | Nxe5 |

Black could have varied with either Qxd4 or Bxe2, but White still gets the advantage—minimal but sure.

(A) If 11. . . . Qxd4, then 12. Nxc6 Qxd1 13. Bxd1 Bxd1 (13. . . . bxc6 14. Ba4!) 14. Nxa7! is good for White.

(B) If 11. . . . Bxe2, then 12. Nxd7 Bxd1 13. Nxf6+ gxf6 14. Rxd1 0-0-0 15. Be3 threatens 16. d5.

| 12 | dxe5 | Bxe2 |

On 12. . . . Qxd1, White impresses with 13. Bxd1! Bxd1 14. Rxd1 Nd7 15. Nb5, and Black's defense on the queen-side seems futile.

13.	Qxe2	Nd5
14.	Nxd5	Qxd5
15.	Rd1	Qa5
16.	Bg5!	. . .

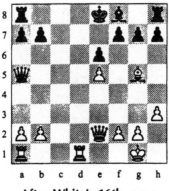

After White's 16th move

16.	**. . .**	**Be7**

White for choice after either:

(A) 16. . . . h6 17. Qd3! Qc7 (17. . . . Qa4 18. Qd8+) 18. Rac1.

(B) 16. . . . f6 17. exf6 Qxg5 18. Qxe6+ Be7 19. Qxe7#.

17.	**Bxe7**	**Kxe7**
18.	**Qg4!**	**Qxe5**
19.	**Qb4+**	**Kf6**

The king must come out. If 19. . . . Ke8, then 20. Qxb7 has the barbarians at the gate.

20.	**Rd7**	**. . .**

Threatens Qb4-e7+, Qe7xf7, and probably other ruinous things.

20.	**. . .**	**Rhf8**
21.	**Re1!**	**. . .**

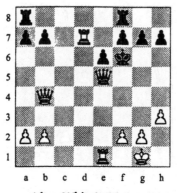

After White's 21st move

21.	. . .	Qb8
22.	Qh4 +	Kg6
23.	Qg4 +	Kf6

Black was unable to avert White's foray and resigned (**1-0**) after White's 24th move.

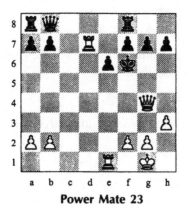

Power Mate 23

Q23: What is White's trenchant mate in two?

POWER GAME *24*

Sveshnikov vs. Sherbakov
USSR, 1991

Exchanging to induce weaknesses, White gradually moves in by attacking them. Stepping and sidling, White doubles on the a1-h8 diagonal with queen and bishop. Black thinks he's okay because of the obstructing d4-knight, but misses a threat, which conceals a most surprising mate. What would life be without surprises?

Sicilian Defense B30

1.	e4	c5
2.	Nf3	...

An unexpected second move. Sveshnikov is a devout practitioner of 2. c3.

2.	...	Nc6
3.	Bb5	e6
4.	0-0	Nge7
5.	c3	a6
6.	Ba4	b5
7.	Bc2	d5

When playing the black side, Sveshnikov has preferred 7. . . . Bb7, delaying d7-d5 for a few moves. But here he has White.

8.	e5	d4

Threatening to trap the bishop with 9. . . . d3 10. Bb3 c4.

9.	Be4	Bb7

After Black's 9th move

| 10. | a4! | ... |

Targeting the b5-pawn, trying to spawn holes in Black's queenside pawn structure.

10.	...	Ng6
11.	axb5	axb5
12.	Rxa8	Bxa8
13.	Na3	Na7

After Black's 13th move

If 13. . . . Ncxe5, then 14. Bxa8 Qxa8 15. Nxe5 Nxe5 16. cxd4 cxd4 17. Nxb5 gives White a distinct edge, so Black decides to hang onto b5.

14.	Bxa8	Qxa8
15.	Qb3	Qb7
16.	cxd4	cxd4
17.	Nxd4	Bxa3
18.	bxa3	Nxe5
19.	Bb2	Nc4

After Black's 19th move

20.	Qg3!	...

The winning move. Now if 20. . . . Nxb2, then 21. Qxg7
Rf8 22. Nxe6! Qe7 23. Nxf8 Qxf8 24. Qxb2, picking off the
errant knight.

20.	...	0-0
21.	Bc3	...

Preserves the bishop from exchange and readies a discovery
with the knight.

21.	...	g6

The idea of closing the long diagonal, 21. . . . e5, invites
the variation 22. Nf5 f6 23. d3 Nb6 24. Bb4 Rb8 25. Be7
g6 26. Bxf6, winning.

22.	d3	Nb6
23.	Qe5	...

An ominous coupling on the long diagonal. Black must cede
the e-pawn by f7-f6 to close the pipeline.

23.   ...   Nd7?

This allows certain mate. Clearly, Black missed the threat
or he would have accepted the consequences and played
23. . . . f6. White played his 24th move and Black resigned
(1-0).

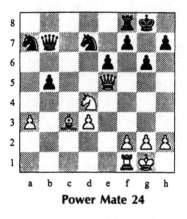

Power Mate 24

Q24: What infernal devilry did White materialize?

POWER GAME **25**

J. Polgar vs. P. Angelova
Thessaloniki, 1988

Black starts off in error, capturing the wrong way. White immediately tries to build a lead in development while fighting fiercely for the dark squares. Black then "wins" a piece, but surrenders her dark-square bishop, and White squats on the vulnerable squares. The defender blinks at the threat, a murderous queen sacrifice, but seeing it wouldn't have helped.

Sicilian Defense, Rossolimo Variation B31

1.	e4	c5
2.	Nf3	Nc6
3.	Bb5	g6
4.	0-0	Bg7
5.	c3	e5

After Black's 5th move

The rule of thumb is that when White plays c2-c3, preparing d2-d4 or d3-d4, Black should strike at the e4-pawn with

Ng8-f6 and/or d7-d5. The text is meant to deter d2-d4, but it doesn't.

6.	d4	exd4
7.	cxd4	Nxd4?

This is not as good a trade as 7. . . . cxd4, though White still gets a fine game after 8. Bf4.

8.	Nxd4	cxd4

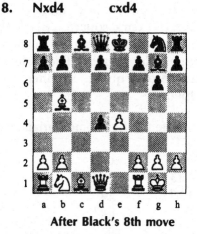

After Black's 8th move

To keep White's knight from c3. If 8. . . . Bxd4, then 9. Nc3 Ne7 10. Bh6, exploiting g7's sudden vacancy to prevent castling.

9.	e5!	...

Also good is 9. f4 Ne7 10. f5.

9.	...	Ne7

Obviously, 9. . . . Bxe5 10. Re1, pinning the bishop, is out of the question. Meanwhile, White has laid a claim to the dark squares.

10.	Bg5	0-0
11.	Qxd4	Nc6
12.	Qh4	Qb6
13.	Nc3	Bxe5

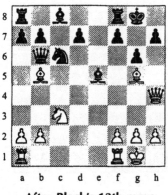

After Black's 13th move

White stands tall after either 13. . . . Nxe5 14. Be7 Re8 15. Nd5 Qxb5 16. Nc7 or 13. . . . d5 14. Bf6 Nxe5 15. Nxd5 Qxb5 16. Qh6! (if 16. . . . Bxh6, then 17. Ne7#).

> **14. Rae1!**   ...

White offers a piece to entice Black into surrendering her flanked bishop, leaving the dark squares susceptible.

> **14.**   ...   **Bxc3**
> **15.**   **bxc3**   **Qxb5**

Black has a piece, but White has a mating attack.

> **16. Qh6**   **Qf5**

To stop 17. Bf6. If 16. . . . f6 (or 16. . . . f5), then 17. Bxf6 Rxf6 18. Re8+ forces mate. White now played her 17th move and Black gave up **(1-0)**, unable to prevent mate.

Power Mate 25

Q25: What savage demolisher did White unleash?

*P*OWER GAME *26*

J. Polgar vs. Metodiev
Albena, 1986

White sets up a standard Yugoslav Attack against the Dragon Sicilian, but Black meshes two different systems with the virtues of neither. White seizes space, war is declared, White's pieces invade, and a rook sacrifice undercuts the kingside pawns. Field Marshal Polgar concludes with an artful queen-and-knight mate.

Sicilian Defense B35

1.	e4	c5
2.	Nf3	Nc6
3.	d4	cxd4
4.	Nxd4	Nf6
5.	Nc3	g6

After Black's 5th move

6.	Be3	...

In this accelerated version of the Dragon, White can get a strong initiative by 6. Nxc6 bxc6 7. e5. But young Judit eschews the opening niceties and forges straight for the Yugoslav Attack.

	6.	. . .	a6

Black is confusing opening systems, a sure recipe for disaster. The text is a Paulsen move. Correct would be 6. . . . d6, a Dragon move.

7.	Bc4	Bg7
8.	Bb3	0-0
9.	f3	Qc7
10.	Qd2	e6

Another Paulsen move, controlling d5. In the Dragon, Black has to play d7-d6 to control e5.

11.	0-0-0	b5

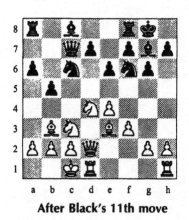

After Black's 11th move

White's development is complete and she's ready to implement the four-part Yugoslav Attack:
  (1) Open the h-file.
  (2) Trade off the defending g7-bishop.
  (3) Drive off the defending f6-knight.
  (4) Mate.

12.	h4	Na5
13.	h5	Nc4

| 14. | Bxc4 | bxc4 |
| 15. | hxg6 | fxg6 |

Part one's mission is accomplished.

| 16. | Bh6 | Rf7 |
| 17. | Bxg7 | Rxg7 |

Rack up part two. The dark squares are there for the taking.

18.	Qg5	Rf7
19.	e5	Nd5
20.	Nxd5	exd5

After Black's 20th move

And there's part three. Everything is go for part four—mate.

| 21. | Rxh7! | Rxh7 |

If 21. . . . Kxh7, then 22. Rh1+, with the following possibilities:

(A) if 22. . . . Kg7, then 23. Qh6+ Kg8 24. Qh8#.
(B) if 22. . . . Kg8, then 23. Qxg6+ Rg7 24. Qe8#.
(C) if 23. . . . Kf8, then 24. Rh8+ Ke7 and White mates in two moves.

| 22. | Qxg6+ | Kh8 |

On 22. . . . Rg7, there follows 23. Qe8+ Kh7 24. Rh1#. White now played her 23rd move and Black resigned (**1-0**).

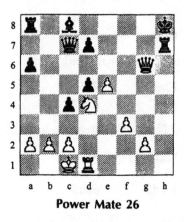

Power Mate 26

Q26: Can you Polgarize mate in two moves?

*P*OWER GAME *27*

Tal vs. NN
Berlin, 1974

White wedges a great pawn at e5, dislodges the f6-knight, and cocks the d3-bishop. A classic bishop sacrifice bludgeons the king's position. Aha! White's rook shifts to the h-file, his knight invades, and his queen comes up. The queenly Black counterpart is deflected, and along comes ceremonious mate. Just another Tal story.

Sicilian Defense B42

1.	e4	c5
2.	Nf3	e6
3.	d4	cxd4
4.	Nxd4	a6
5.	Bd3	Nf6
6.	0-0	Qc7
7.	Kh1	d6
8.	f4	Nbd7

After Black's 8th move

9.	Nd2	. . .

Normally the knight comes out to c3. Against Black's quiet
Paulsen setup, White does not have to hurry. So Tal develops
it to d2, en route to f3, where the knight will support the
advance e4-e5.

9.	...	Be7
10.	N2f3	0-0
11.	Qe2	Nc5
12.	e5	dxe5
13.	fxe5	Nfd7
14.	Bg5	Nxe5?

Tal frankly admits he overlooked this capture. Fortunately
for him, it's a mistake. Better would be 14. . . . Nb6, where
Black is still breathing.

15.	Bxe7	Nxf3

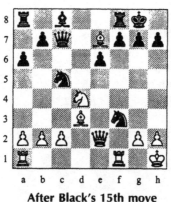

After Black's 15th move

This zwischenzug threatens mate at h2. There are four ways
to capture this knight. Which is best?

16.	Rxf3!	...

This answers the question and readies the rook for rambling
and rumbling.

16.	...	Qxe7

After Black's 16th move

| 17. | Bxh7 + ! | . . . |

Greco's classic bishop sacrifice. But there's a twist.

| 17. | . . . | Kxh7 |
| 18. | Rh3 + | Kg8 |

If 18. . . . Kg6, then 19. Qh5 + Kf6 20. Rf3#.

| 19. | Nf5! | . . . |

The intrusion 19. Qh5? fails to 19. . . . f6, and Black defends.

| 19. | . . . | Qg5 |

White now played his determining 20th move and Black resigned (**1-0**).

Power Mate 27

Q27: How did White polish off his opponent?

*P*OWER GAME *28*

Luther vs. Varga
Germany-Hungary Match, 1991

Black goes with a flank advance and White counters with a central riposte. Triple pawn targets are instilled in Black's kingside, and the exchange is sacrificed against them. White's arrayed bishops scourge the kingside, catching Black's queen off guard in an impossible overload. The king is dumped.

Sicilian Defense B47

1.	e4	c5
2.	Nf3	e6
3.	d4	cxd4
4.	Nxd4	Nc6
5.	Nc3	Qc7
6.	Be2	a6
7.	0-0	Nf6
8.	Kh1	b5

After Black's 8th move

This move at this point in this variation has a dubious reputation. Authorities who publish their ideas prefer 8. . . . . Bb4 or 8. . . . Nxd4.

9.	Nxc6	dxc6
10.	f4	b4
11.	e5	bxc3
12.	exf6	gxf6
13.	bxc3	. . .

The book move is 13. Qe1, as in the games Velimirovic-Damjanovic, Sombor, 1972, and Short-Ljubojevic, Linares, 1995. In both encounters, White got the advantage after working his queen to h4.

13.	. . .	c5
14.	Bf3	Rb8
15.	Be3	Bd6
16.	Qd3	0-0

Not 16. . . . Bxf4? because of 17. Bxf4 Qxf4 18. Bc6 + .

17.	Rad1	Rb6

After Black's 17th move

Capturing on f4 is not any better here: 17. . . . Bxf4? 18. Bxf4 Qxf4 19. Be4 Qh4 20. Bxh7 + Qxh7 21. Qg3 + and 22. Qxb8.

18. f5!   ...

White pushes ahead to open lines of attack against the black king.

18. ...   exf5

If Black strays with 18. . . . Bxh2 19. Bh6 Qg3, White wins spectacularly with 20. Qd8!!, and f8 is woefully piteous.

19. Bh6   Re8
20. Bd5   ...

Clearing the f-file while posting the bishop imperiously.

20. ...   Kh8

After Black's 20th move

21. Rxf5!   Bxf5?

A tougher, Russian-winter defense is offered by 20. . . . Be5.

22. Qxf5   Qe7?

The final error. After 22. . . . Qd8 Black can still resist. Now the black queen finds itself left with too many responsibilities. White played his 23rd move and Black resigned (**1-0**).

Power Mate 28

Q28: How can White make capital of Black's pathetic queen?

Kasparov vs. Kengis
Riga, 1995

In a sharp position, White plies his king to the side and vigorously pushes the f-pawn. Rooks double behind it, and a disruptive bishop sacrifice on f6 bars defense. Victory is convoyed through by an armada of major pieces before the defending ships reach the shadow line. It's mate, even on the high seas.

Sicilian Defense B47

1.	e4	c5
2.	Nf3	e6
3.	d4	cxd4
4.	Nxd4	Nc6
5.	Nc3	Qc7
6.	Be2	a6
7.	0-0	Nf6
8.	Kh1	. . .

Not 8. f4?, because of 8. . . . Nxd4 9. Qxd4 Bc5, pinning the unfortunate queen.

8.	. . .	Nxd4
9.	Qxd4	Bc5
10.	Qd3	h5?!

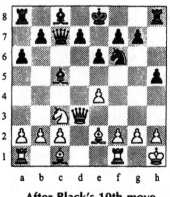

After Black's 10th move

Coffeehouse chess. An attack on White's king in this situation, without any real support, can hardly succeed against correct play. Later, Black pays dearly for weakening his kingside.

| | 11. | Bg5 | ... |

Right on. White just develops, ignoring Black's threat and setting up a threat of his own.

| | 11. | ... | b5 |

Here, and also later, 11. . . . Ng4 is met by 12. f4 Nf2+ 13. Rxf2 Bxf2 14. e5 and 15. Ne4. White's initiative, his lead in development, and his control of space more than offset the loss of the exchange.

| | 12. | f4 | Bb7 |

If 12. . . . b4, then 13. e5 bxc3 14. exf6 cxb2 15. fxg7 bxal/Q 16. Rxal Rg8 17. Qh7 wins for White.

| | 13. | e5! | ... |

Kasparov's improvement over 13. Bf3.

	13.	...	Nd5
	14.	Nxd5	Bxd5
	15.	a4?!	...

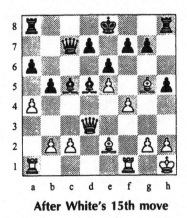

After White's 15th move

Highbrow chess. Kasparov wants to confuse his opponent by creating tension on both flanks. Simply 15. Bf3 entitles White to keep the initiative. Now Black gets unwarranted counterplay.

15.	...	Qc6!
16.	Bf3	Bxf3
17.	Rxf3	bxa4!
18.	f5	Rb8!
19.	Raf1	0-0?

After Black's 19th move

Black should have followed through with his idea, 19. . . . Rxb2. After 20. fxe6 Qxe6 21. Rxf7 Qxf7 22. Rxf7 Kxf7 23.

h4 a3!, the passed a-pawn keeps White at bay. The text, looking to safeguard the king, actually places the king in danger.

	20.	Bf6!	Qb5

The line 20. . . . gxf6 21. Rg3+ Kh8 22. Qe2 is hopeless. And 20. . . . Rb4, trying to defend along the fourth rank, succumbs after 21. Bxg7! Kxg7 22. Rg3+ Rg4 23. f6+ Kh6 24. Qd2+ Kg6 25. Qf4!

	21.	Rg3!	. . .

Inviting 21. . . . Qxd3 22. Rxg7+ Kh8 23. Rg5+ Kh7 24. Rxh5+ Kg8 25. Rh8#. Black sidesteps, but the position can't be retrieved.

	21.	. . .	g6
	22.	Qd1!	exf5
	23.	Rxf5	Rb6
	24.	Qxh5	

Here Black resigned (1-0).

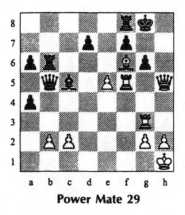

Power Mate 29

Q29: After the likely continuation 24. . . . Rxf6 25. exf6 Re8, how does White force checkmate?

*P*OWER GAME *30*

Hector vs. Mortensen
Reykjavik, 1995

Forcing exchanges lead to an opened middle. Black's king is pinned down in the center. A forbidding rook occupies the seventh rank and Black's king has to run. Queen, rook, knight, and pawn coalesce into an allied force, pursue the big guy, and blanket him in mate.

Sicilian Defense B48

1.	e4	c5
2.	Nf3	Nc6
3.	d4	cxd4
4.	Nxd4	Qc7
5.	Nc3	e6
6.	Be3	a6
7.	Bd3	b5
8.	0-0	Bb7
9.	Nb3	Ne5?!

After Black's 9th move

A move with a poor reputation in this particular position. Thus far, attempts at rehabilitation have not worked. It enables the knight to transfer to c4 but at the expense of initiative. Better is 9. . . . d6 or 9. . . . Nf6.

	10.	f4	...

Also serviceable is 10. Qe2 Nf6 11. f4 Nc4 12. Bd4 (Georghiu-Sax, Bucharest, 1967).

	10.	...	Nc4
	11.	Bd4!	d6

The capture 11. . . . Nxb2 can be met by 12. Nxb5!

	12.	Qe2!	...

Planning to undermine the knight by 13. a4. Black decides to strike in the center, but with his king still uncastled, it's a dangerous business.

	12.	...	e5
	13.	Nd5!	...

Intruding on the vulnerable d5-square, leading to the unveiling of the e-file by exchange.

	13.	...	Bxd5
	14.	exd5	Be7
	15.	fxe5	dxe5
	16.	Bxc4	exd4

After Black's 16th move

17. **d6!** . . .

The position is sufficiently open, and now the combinations begin.

17. . . . **Qxc4**
18. **Qf3!** . . .

White avoids the queen exchange with a gain of time, menacing the rook at a8.

18. . . . **Rb8**

This prevents a later Qb7. If 18. . . . . Rd8, then 19. Na5 Qe6 20. dxe7 Nxe7 21. Rae1 Qd5 22. Nc6 Qxf3 23. Rxe7 + wins.

19. **Rae1!** . . .

Increasing the pressure with an annoying pin. The e7-bishop won't run away.

19. . . . **Nf6**
20. **Rxe7 +** . . .

This appropriates the seventh rank with a gain of time. Now f7 becomes a real target.

20. . . . **Kf8**
21. **Na5** **Qc5**
22. **Qb3!** . . .

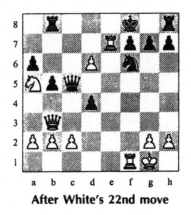

After White's 22nd move

Also good enough was 22. Nb7. For example, if 22. . . . Qc4, then 23. b3 Qc3 24. Qd5 Qe3+ (24. . . . Nxd5 leads to mate in four moves after 25. Rfxf7+) 25. Kh1 Qe6 26. Qxe6 fxe6 27. Nc5.

22.	...	Qh5
23.	Nc6	Rc8
24.	d7	Rd8
25.	Re8+	

Here Black resigned (1-0).

Power Mate 30

Q30: Can you illustrate how White mates from the final position?

POWER GAME *31*

Alberston vs. NN
New York, 1995

Curiously, Black surrenders the middle without a fight.
White builds steadily in the center and eyes the kingside.
Black, moreover, is too slow in creating counterplay, and
misses his last chance. An undignified pawn mate ensues.

Sicilian Defense B50

1.	e4	c5
2.	Nf3	d6
3.	Bc4	...

After White's 3rd move

This is supposed to be harmless, but when Black neglects
to play Ng8-f6, White is given a free hand to take over
the center.

3.	...	Nc6
4.	0-0	g6
5.	c3	Bg7

6.	d4	cxd4
7.	cxd4	e6
8.	Nc3	Nge7
9.	Bg5	0-0

After Black's 9th move

White has everything he could hope for out of the opening: better center, better development, safer king, etc.

10.	Qd2	Re8

Black plays to preserve his dark-square bishop from exchanges. However, the weakening of f7 tells later on.

11.	Bh6	Bh8
12.	Rad1	...

More accurate would be 12. Rfe1, to prevent d6-d5. But Black continues to play on the flank.

12.	...	a6

What has this got to do with the price of tea in China? Black should have risked defeat for counterplay with 12. . . . d5.

13.	Qf4	b5?

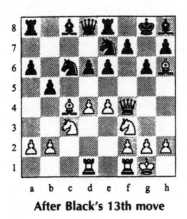

After Black's 13th move

Last chance for 13. . . . d6-d5.

       14.   Ng5!   ...

White's attack is unstoppable. If 14. . . . f6, then 15. Nxe6.
The best chance is 14. . . . Rf8, dumping the exchange.

       14.   ...   **Nf5**

Clever, but insufficient. Now White's e-pawn goes on a
rampage.

       15.   exf5   **bxc4**
       16.   fxg6   **f5**

White now silenced Black with his 17th move (**1-0**).

Power Mate 31

Q31: What was White's irresistible rejoinder?

POWER GAME *32*

Kupreicik vs. Tukmakov
Riga, 1985

White commandeers space, first by advancing the f-pawn
and later by moving up the d-pawn. Black becomes cramped
and is unable to prevent White's invasion force from maneuvering in on the kingside. Ignoring feeble threats, White
instigates both his rooks while Black's stumbling troop can't
avert a mighty tripling on the h-file. It's mate, plain and
simple.

Sicilian Defense B74

1.	e4	c5
2.	Nf3	Nc6
3.	d4	cxd4
4.	Nxd4	Nf6
5.	Nc3	d6
6.	f4	g6
7.	Be2	Bg7
8.	Nb3	0-0
9.	Be3	Be6
10.	0-0	Na5

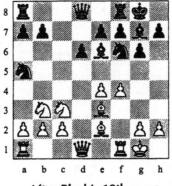

After Black's 10th move

Black opts for an older main line. The modern approach is
10. . . . Rc8. If White continues with 11. f5, Black retreats,
11. . . . Bd7, and follows with Nc6-e5.

11.	f5	. . .

This grabs space and launches the assault.

11.	. . .	Bc4
12.	Bd3	Bxd3
13.	cxd3	Nc6

The book line is 13. . . . d5, which theory gives as offering
equal chances.

14.	d4	Rc8
15.	Qf3	Nd7

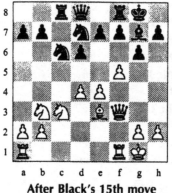

After Black's 15th move

A recommended move here is 15. . . . e6. With 15. . . .
Nd7, Black looks to bring this knight to the queenside.
Meanwhile, withdrawing the knight to d7 enables White to
obtain serious kingside chances.

16.	Rad1	Nb6
17.	Bg5	Qd7
18.	Qh3	a5
19.	Bh6	Qe8
20.	Rf4	. . .

A rook lift before storming the beach.

20.   ...   a4

After Black's 20th move

21.   Rh4   Bf6

If Black plays 21. . . . axb3, there follows 22. Bxg7 Kxg7 23. Rxh7+ Kf6 24. Qh4+ g5 25. Qh6#. Nor does 23. . . . Kg8 provide escape because of 24. Qh6.

22.   Bg5   Bxg5

No better is 22. . . . h5. After 23. Rxh5 gxh5 24. Bxf6 exf6 25. Rd3, mate is soon delivered by heavy pieces along the g- and h-files.

23.   Rxh7   Bf6

If 23. . . . axb3, then 24. Rh8+ Kg7 25. f6+ Kxf6 (capturing on f6 with anything else allows immediate mate) 26. e5+ Nxe5 27. Ne4+ Kg7 28. Qh7#.

24.   Qh6   ...

For the curious, White is threatening 25. e5 dxe5 26. Ne4. Black's next move is practically forced.

24.   ...   e5
25.   Rd3

A final rook rise, and Black resigned (**1-0**).

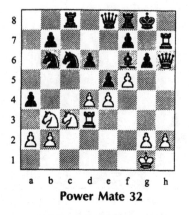

Power Mate 32

Q32: If Black responds 25. . . . exd4, how does White compose a checkmate?

*P*OWER GAME *33*

Verduga vs. Hernao
Bayamo, 1990

The players castle on opposite sides to wage all-out warfare, but White starts a pawn storm and opens lines for penetration. Several sacrifices follow, including one by Black. Still, it's the first mover who gets there first. In the finale, Black is beaten to the punch, and punched and beaten, along the h-file.

Sicilian Defense B78

1.	e4	c5
2.	Nf3	d6
3.	d4	cxd4
4.	Nxd4	Nf6
5.	Nc3	g6
6.	Be3	Bg7
7.	f3	Nc6
8.	Qd2	0-0
9.	Bc4	Bd7
10.	g4	Rc8
11.	Bb3	Ne5
12.	0-0-0	Nc4
13.	Bxc4	Rxc4
14.	h4	Qa5

After Black's 14th move

A sharp position, characteristic of the Yugoslav Dragon. The players castle on opposite sides and take aim at the opponent's king.

| 15. | Kb1 | ... |

The usual move is 15. Nb3, deflecting Black's queen from the defense of e5.

| 15. | ... | Rfc8 |
| 16. | h5 | Bxg4 |

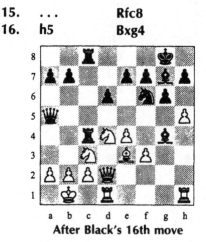

After Black's 16th move

Black plays this sacrifice in the wrong move order. He should first play 16. . . . Rxc3!, and after 17. bxc3, come back with 17. . . . Bxg4!.

| 17. | hxg6 | ... |

Taking the bishop, 17. fxg4?, would be a clear mistake here because of 17. . . . Rxc3! 18. bxc3 Nxe4. After White saves his queen, Black continues with the destructive 19. . . . Nxc3+.

| 17. | ... | hxg6 |
| 18. | Bh6 | ... |

On 18. fxg4 there follows the familiar exchange sacrifice on c3.

| 18. | ... | Bh8 |

White was threatening 19. Bxg7 Kxg7 20. Qh6+.

| 19. | fxg4 | ... |

Now this recapture is okay.

| 19. | ... | Rxc3 |

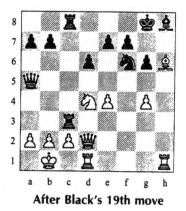

After Black's 19th move

| 20. | Nf5! | Qd8 |

Black's defense gives in after 20. . . . Nxe4 21. Nxe7+ Kh7 22. Bf8+. Even the queen sacrifice 22. . . . Qh5 allows 23. Qh6+! Qxh6 24. Rxh6#. On the other hand, 20. . . . gxf5 leads to debasing mate after 21. Qg5+ Kh7 22. Bf8+.

| 21. | Bg5 | ... |

The threat is 22. Rxh8+ Kxh8 23. Bxf6+ exf6 24. Rh1+ Kg8 25. Qh6.

21.	...	gxf5

White played a winning breakthrough and Black resigned on his 23rd move (**1-0**).

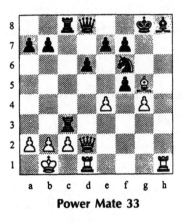

Power Mate 33

Q33: How does White prestidigitate mate?

POWER GAME *34*

Patrici vs. Torres
Correspondence, 1973

Black treads the wrong path, throwing away his center for a wing pawn. His queen suffers being misplaced, and White besieges it to gain time for combat. Hammering away at f6 with a rook hit, White catches Black in a stupor, and three pieces lay him to rest.

Sicilian Defense B83

1.	e4	c5
2.	Nf3	d6
3.	d4	cxd4
4.	Nxd4	Nf6
5.	Nc3	e6
6.	Be2	Nc6
7.	Be3	Be7
8.	0-0	0-0
9.	f4	Nxd4

After Black's 9th move

Usually in the Scheveningen, Black inserts a7-a6 right about here. If he doesn't want to play 9. . . . a6, then his choices are 9. . . . Qc7, 9. . . . e5, 9. . . . Bd7, and the text, 9. . . . Nxd4, the weakest of the four.

| 10. | Bxd4 | . . . |

Good also is 10. Qxd4.

| 10. | . . . | a6 |

Kavalek, who has played this position as Black on several occasions, preferred 10. . . . b6, followed by Bc8-b7. The text is unnecessary and therefore a loss of time.

| 11. | Qe1 | e5? |

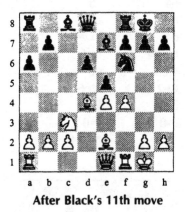

After Black's 11th move

Here Black attempts a combination, but the idea is unsound.

| 12. | fxe5 | dxe5 |
| 13. | Bxe5 | Qb6 + |

This pilfers a pawn, but is it wise to remove the queen from play so?

| 14. | Kh1 | Qxb2 |
| 15. | Qg3 | . . . |

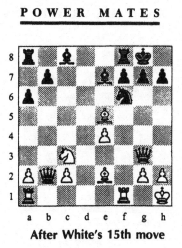

After White's 15th move

White's multi-purpose move guards the e5-bishop, pins the g7-pawn, threatens Nc3-d5, and there's not too much Black can do about it.

	15. . . .	Kh8

Or 15. . . . Qxc2 16. Bxf6 Bxf6 17. Rxf6, winning a piece because of the pin.

16.	Nd5	Qxc2
17.	Nxe7	Qxe2

Black has managed to keep the number of pieces even, but White's next move puts the situation in proper perspective.

	18. Rxf6!	. . .

The rook is immune from capture: 18. . . . gxf6 19. Bxf6#.

	18. . . .	Qxe4

If Black had really wanted to play on, he should have tried 18. . . . Qg4, conceding a losing endgame. The text allows a pretty finish. White now played and forced mate on his 20th move (**1-0**).

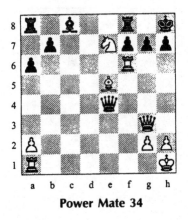

Power Mate 34

Q34: How does White detonate destiny in two moves?

*P*OWER GAME *35*

Adorjan vs. Ribli
Budapest, 1979

The day dawns with the players castling on opposite sides, expecting a big battle. Black dilly-dallies, but White mobilizes appropriately, backing up the g- and h-pawns with bellicose rooks. The pawns advance, the g-file is cleared, and White doubles major pieces, queen first. A mating sacrifice follows, on the very square Black thought he had covered. Gone the day and all its imagined sweets.

Sicilian Defense B90

1.	e4	c5
2.	Nf3	d6
3.	d4	cxd4
4.	Nxd4	Nf6
5.	Nc3	a6
6.	Be3	e5
7.	Nb3	Be6
8.	Qd2	Nbd7
9.	f3	Rc8

After Black's 9th move

The preference these days is for 9. . . . b5 or 9. . . . Be7, leaving the rook on a8.

10.	**g4**	**Be7**
11.	**0-0-0**	**Nb6?**

A double error, so to speak. First, Black should have tried to slow down White's kingside initiative by 11. . . . h6. Then 12. . . . b5 should be employed to generate counterplay on the queenside.

12.	**h4!**	**...**

Adorjan's improvement. An immediate 12. g5 can be answered by 12. . . . Nh5, so White should follow the plan 13. h5 and then 14. g5.

12.	**...**	**0-0**
13.	**h5!**	**Nc4**

After Black's 13th move

The attempt to break out in the center with 13. . . . d5 is refuted by Adorjan as follows: 14. Bxb6 Qxb6 15. g5 d4 16. Na4 Qc6 17. gxf6 gxf6 18. Nac5! Bxc5 19. Rg1 + Kh8 20. Qh6 and wins.

14.	**Bxc4**	**Rxc4**
15.	**g5**	**Nd7**

16.	Rdg1!	Qc7
17.	g6	Rc8

After Black's 17th move

Ribli refuses to take anything, keeping the lines closed, making it harder for White to penetrate.

18.	Bh6!	Bf6

Still refusing to capture, but now White insists.

19.	gxh7 +	Kxh7
20.	Bxg7!	Bxg7
21.	h6!	. . .

But not the tempting 21. Rxg7 + ? because of 21. . . . Kxg7 22. Qg5 + Kf8 23. h6 Qd8!, and Black is alive.

21.	. . .	Bf6

Both 21. . . . Bf8 and 21. . . . Bh8 are met by 22. Qg5.

22.	Qg2!

Black (hold, enough!) here resigned (**1-0**).

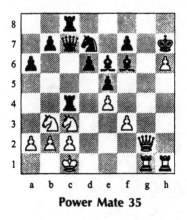

Power Mate 35

Q35: How does White deliver mate?

POWER GAME 36

Pedersen vs. Gallmeyer
Denmark, 1971

Maneuvering to exploit the weakened queenside, White gradually improves his piece placements, threat by threat. His forces become so well coordinated that he is able to sacrifice his queen in order to maintain the active line. The combined efforts of rooks and minor pieces beset the black king, who is mated when betrayed by the lack of harmony in his own regiments.

Sicilian Defense B96

1.	e4	c5
2.	Nf3	d6
3.	d4	cxd4
4.	Nxd4	Nf6
5.	Nc3	a6
6.	Bg5	e6
7.	f4	b5
8.	e5	dxe5
9.	fxe5	Qc7
10.	exf6	Qe5 +
11.	Be2	Qxg5
12.	0-0	. . .

After White's 12th move

One of the original main lines of the Polugaevsky Variation. White tries to capitalize on quick development. Today, 12. Qd3 is played more often.

12. ...   Qe5

Not an easy move to find. The text stops the centralization by Nc3-e4 and sets up the pinning Bf8-c5.

13. Bf3   ...

Usurping control of the a8-h1 diagonal, as well as the square c6, weakened by the advance b7-b5.

13. ...   Ra7
14. Nc6!?   ...

A clever shot, giving Black the opportunity to go wrong.

14. ...   Qc5+

Second best. The best would be 14. . . . Nxc6 15. Bxc6+ Bd7 16. Bxd7+ Rxd7 17. Qf3, when 17. . . . Bd6! keeps the game balanced. Black must be careful about overuse of the queen, but it's hard to eschew a time-gaining check.

15. Kh1   Rd7

After Black's 15th move

The surprise is that on 15. . . . Nxc6 White has 16. Ne4!, and Black's queen has no desirable place to go:

(A) 16. . . . Qd4 17. Nd6+! Qxd6 18. fxg7 wins.

(B) 16. . . . Qe5 17. fxg7 Bxg7 (17. . . . Qxg7 18. Nf6+
and 19. Bxc6) 18. Nd6+ Ke7 19. Bxc6; and if 19. . . . Qxd6,
then 20. Rxf7+.

(C) 16. . . . Qb6 17. fxg7 Bxg7 18. Nd6+ Ke7 19. Bxc6
f5 (19. . . . Qxc6 20. Rxf7+) 20. Nxf5+, with a winning
attack; for example, 20. . . . exf5 21. Re1+ Kf7 22. Qd5+
Kg6 23. Qd6+ Bf6 24. Be8+.

	16.	Nxb8!	. . .

Sacrificing the queen for a rook and minor piece in order
to nurture the attack against the uncastled Black king. Let's
see where it goes.

16.	. . .	Rxd1
17.	Raxd1	gxf6

Now Black can play Ke7.

18.	Ne4	Qc7?

This loses in spectacular fashion. The only good move was
18. . . . Qf5!, found by Polugaevsky in 1960, but tucked
away in his secret notebook. Even when he analyzed the B96
section for ECO (1975 edition), he couldn't bring himself to
reveal his analysis. He simply gave the contemporary evalu-
ation, which assumed that White was winning.

19.	Nxf6+	Ke7
20.	Bh5!	. . .

After White's 20th move

There is no answer to this answer.

(A) 20. . . . Qc5 21. Nc6 + ! (1-0, Parr-Klibon, West Germany, 1967); and if 21. . . . Qxc6, then 22. Ng8 + Rxg8 23. Rxf7 + Ke8 24. Rg7#.

(B) 20. . . . Qxb8 21. Ng8 + Rxg8 (21. . . . Ke8 22. Bxf7#) 22. Rxf7 + Ke8 23. Rg7#.

(C) 20. . . . Bh6 21. Nc6 + ! Kf8 22. Rd8 + Kg7 23. Ne8 + Rxe8 24. Rxf7 + Kg8 25. Rxe8 + Bf8 26. Rexf8#.

20.	**...**	**Bg7**
21.	**Nc6 + !**	**Qxc6**

Or 21. . . . Kf8 22. Nd7 + , and there are mates wherever Black turns:

(A) 22. . . . Kg8 23. Ne7#;.

(B) 22. . . . Qxd7 23. Rxd7 Bxd7 24. Rxf7 + Ke8 (24. . . . Kg8 25. Ne7#) 25. Rf6#.

White fired three more salvos and Black resigned on his 24th move **(1-0)**.

Power Mate 36

Q36: What chessic funeral arrangements did White make for his opponent?

POWER GAME *37*

Aianski vs. Donchev
Varna, 1977

White pushes the e-pawn to gain more space, but it proves to be premature, and Black asserts against it. Since the center stays blocked, Black opts to remain uncastled, pursuing a kingside attack. The h-file becomes unobstructed, and when White fails to dissipate the aggresion by trading queens, he walks into an unveiling that unites diagonal and file in mate.

King's Indian Attack C00

1.	e4	e6
2.	d3	d5
3.	Nd2	Nf6
4.	Ngf3	b6
5.	g3	Bb7

After Black's 5th move

6.	e5	. . .

This advance is effective after Black has castled kingside. Here, Black's pressure on e4 forces White to make an impulsive decision. The alternative was 6. Bg2, and if 6. . . . dxe4, then 7. Ng5 regains the pawn. Sometimes a little tactic is needed to maintain a strategic advantage.

6.	. . .	Nfd7
7.	Bg2	c5
8.	0-0	Nc6
9.	Re1	Qc7
10.	Qe2	Be7
11.	c3?	. . .

After White's 11th move

A mistake. White wants to play d3-d4, but there's no time. Better to essay 11. Nf1 or 11. h4.

11.	. . .	g5!

Ready to attack the defending knight with g5-g4. Black, having not yet castled kingside, is free to pursue this line of play. White tries to stop the advance g5-g4, but it can't be done.

12.	h3	h5
13.	Nb3?	. . .

After White's 13th move

White should bolster the kingside by 13. Nf1.

13.	...	g4
14.	hxg4	hxg4
15.	Nh2	Qxe5
16.	Nxg4	...

White is left a pawn behind, with a dismal game, after 16. Qxe5 Ndxe5. The text regains the pawn but allows Black to retain the queen for attack.

16.	...	Qh5
17.	Bf4	d4!
18.	cxd4?	...

The final mistake. It was necessary to play 18. c4.

18.	...	Nxd4!

Winning the queen or forcing mate. Big choice.

19.	Nxd4	...

Black played his 19th move and White resigned (0–1).

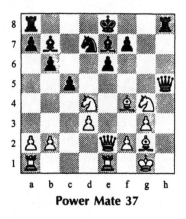

Power Mate 37

Q37: What mate did Black envision and execute?

POWER GAME 38

Muratov vs. Antoshin
USSR, 1964

Each player tries to beat the other to the punch. At first, Black inflicts weaknesses around White's king, which is forced to move back to the center. Meanwhile, White opens the g-file, manages to find shelter for his own king behind the e-pawn, and lulls Black to sleep, so much so that he moves the wrong rook, leaving his king without escape. A clearance sacrifice leads to sure mate with queen and bishop.

French Defense C01

1.	e4	e6
2.	d4	d5
3.	Nc3	Bb4

The Winawer Variation.

4.	exd5	exd5
5.	Qf3	Qe7 + !

This is an improvement on 5. . . . Nc6, Larsen-Portisch, Amsterdam Interzonal, 1964.

6.	Nge2	Nc6
7.	Be3	Nf6

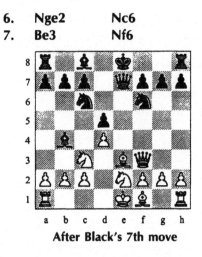

After Black's 7th move

8.	h3	. . .

A necessary preventive move. If 8. 0-0-0?, then 8. . . . Bxc3
9. bxc3 Bg4 10. Qf4 g5! (0-1), Corden-Miles, Oxford 1970.
On 11. Qxg5, there follows 11. . . . Bxe2 12. Bxe2 Qa3+,
with the devastating 13. . . . Ne4 to ensue.

8.	. . .	Ne4

Stronger would be 8. . . . Bxc3 9. bxc3 and then 9. . . .
Ne4. White cannot avert this problem by recapturing with
the knight, 9. Nxc3?, because of 9. . . . Nxd4.

9.	0-0-0	Bxc3
10.	Nxc3	. . .

Now this is possible because the d4-pawn is upheld.

10.	. . .	Nxc3
11.	bxc3	0-0

Black loses too much time with the rapacious 11. . . . Qa3+
12. Kd2 Qxa2. The question is: Are White's queenside pawn
weaknesses exploitable?

12.	Bd3	Be6
13.	Qh5	. . .

Threatening mate in one and thereby provoking a pawn
advance.

13.	. . .	f5
14.	g4!	Na5?!

Safer would be 14. . . . g6 15. Qh6 Qg7.

15.	gxf5	. . .

Opening the g-file for rook assault.

15.	. . .	Qa3+

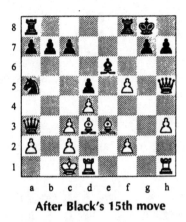

After Black's 15th move

16.   Kd2!   ...

White has correctly judged that his king will be safe enough
in the center. The e3-bishop (and later the e3-pawn) will
provide sufficient cover.

16.   ...   Nc4 +

After Black's 16th move

17.   Ke2   ...

Not 17. Bxc4? because of 17. . . . . Rxf5.

17.	. . .	Bf7
18.	Qh4	Nxe3
19.	fxe3	Rae8

Using the other rook, 19. . . . Rfe8, looks better. At least this keeps f8 vacant.

| 20. | Rdg1 | Qe7 |

White played his 21st move and Black resigned (1-0).

Power Mate 38

Q38: With what jolt did White stagger Black?

P OWER GAME *39*

Survila vs. Skobilkov
USSR, 1978

Black offers White the chance to disrupt his kingside by capturing a knight. White takes it, and Black filches the noxious b-pawn. Sensing greater opportunity, White lets his rook hang so that Black's queen becomes really displaced. By the time Black salvages his queen and menaced bishop, he's forgotten about his king, which succumbs to the diagonal cooperation of White's queen and bishops.

French Defense E02

1.	e4	e6
2.	d4	d5
3.	e5	c5
4.	c3	Nc6
5.	Nf3	Qb6

After Black's 5th move

Lately, 5. . . . . Bd7 is in fashion.

| 6. | Be2 | . . . |

The modern move is 6. a3.

6.   ...   Nh6

Usually Black prefaces this with 6. . . . cxd4 7. cxd4 and
then 7. . . . Nh6, when 8. Bxh6? Qxb2 is perfectly safe.

7.   Bxh6   Qxb2?

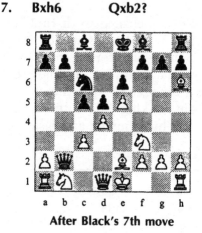

After Black's 7th move

This is supposed to be a mistake, but the reasons why keep
changing. The acceptable line was 7. . . . gxh6.

8.   Be3   ...

The original thought was 8. Bc1 Qxa1 9. Qc2 cxd4 10. 0-0
Bd7 11. Nfd2 Na5 12. Nb3 Nxb3 13. Qxb3 dxc3 14. Nxc3
d4 15. Nb5, and White is winning.

The verdict was challenged in Payne-Plesse, West Germany, 1973, where Black introduced 11. . . . dxc3! (instead
of 11. . . . Na5) 12. Nb3 (12. Nxc3? Nd4 13. Qd3 Qxc3!—
advantage Black) 12. . . . Nb4 13. Nxa1 Nxc2 14. Nxc2 b5!
15. Ba3 (15. Nxc3 Rc8) 15. . . . a5!, and Black went on to
win in 26 moves.

So 8. Bc1 went from a worthy move (!) to a questionable
one (?), and yet this is not the end of the story. The exclama-
tion point has been restored! Psakhis and Suetin give 8. Bc1!
Qxa1 9. Qc2 cxd4 10. Bb5 (the new idea) 10. . . . Bd7 11.

Bxc6 bxc6 12. Nfd2, closing in on the Black queen. Punctuation is so important.

8.	...	Qxa1
9.	Qc2	cxd4
10.	Nxd4	Nxd4?

An improvement is 10. . . . Bd7 11. 0-0 Nxe5 (Kupreicik-Alburt, USSR, 1970). After 12. Nd2 Qxf1+ 13. Kxf1, material is about even and a definitive assessment is yet to be made.

| 11. | Bxd4 | Ba3 |

After Black's 11th move

This move has to come in before White castles. If Black delays, White just plays 12. 0-0 and 13. Nd2; and if he gets more time, 13. Rd1 and 14. c4.

| 12. | Bb5+! | Kd8 |

The alternatives are pretty dismal:

(A) 12. . . . Bd7 13. Bxd7+ Kxd7 14. 0-0 Qb2 15. Qa4+ b5 16. Qa6 and White is ahead.

(B) 12. . . . Kf8 13. 0-0 Qb2 14. Bc5+! Kg8 15. Nxa3, and White wears the emperor's clothes (after dry cleaning).

| 13. | 0-0 | Qb2 |
| 14. | Qa4 | Be7? |

Or 14. . . . Bf8 15. Qa5+ b6 16. Bxb6+ axb6. 17. Qxb6+ Ke7 18. Qd6#. White now forced Black's resignation, playing the first move of a mate in three **(1-0)**.

Power Mate 39

Q39: How does White force mate in three?

POWER GAME *40*

Ilievsky vs. Graul
Sandomierz, 1976

White develops at the enemy queen's expense, building an easy game. Using the center as a springboard, White forces Black to weaken his kingside and transfers the attack there. After readying the final assault with a rook lift, White furthers his aims by encamping his dark-square bishop. Black misses the import of these moves and blunders into the sacrificial rite of mate.

French Defense C10

1.	e4	e6
2.	d4	d5
3.	Nd2	dxe4
4.	Nxe4	Nf6

The usual move here is 4. . . . Nd7. The text has a bad reputation.

5.	Nxf6+	...

Best. Now Black is forced to play either 5. . . . gxf6, ruining his pawns, or 5. . . . Qxf6, exposing the queen.

5.	...	Qxf6

After Black's 5th move

	6.	Nf3	Bd6

More fight-back is offered by 6. . . . h6.

	7.	Bg5	Qf5

Already we see that Black may wind up losing too much time because of the repeated need to move his queen.

	8.	Bd3	Qa5 +

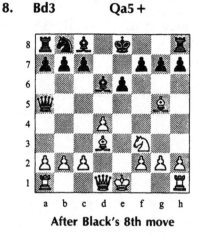

After Black's 8th move

	9.	c3	Nd7
	10.	0-0	c6
	11.	Re1	Qc7

Had the queen stayed on d8, it could have reached c7 in one move instead of four.

| | 12. | Qe2 | 0-0 |

After Black's 12th move

White has a massive lead in development, coupled with a large advantage in space. With his next move, he provokes the decisive weakness.

| | 13. | Qe4 | g6 |

The only way to parry the mate threat, but now f6 and h6 require constant care.

| | 14. | Qh4 | Re8 |
| | 15. | Re4 | Nb6? |

15. . . . b6 and 16. . . . Bb7 must be better than the text. Even if Black touched his knight and had to move it, 15. . . . Nf8 would be better.

| | 16. | Bf6 | . . . |

Entering the wound. There is no defense.

(A) 16. . . . Bf8 17. Qxh7+ Kxh7 18. Rh4+ Bh6 19. Ng5+ Kg8 20. Rxh6 and mate on h8.

(B) 16. . . . h5 (the best try) 17. Re5! (the right answer, threatening 18. Rxh5) 17. . . . Bxe5 18. dxe5! Nd5 19. Qg5 Nxf6 (19. . . . Kh7 20. Qxh5+) 20. exf6 Qd6 21. Bxg6! Qf8

22. Ne5 fxg6 23. Qxg6+ Kh8 24. Nf7+ Qxf7 25. Qxf7 Rg8
26. Qxh5#.

16.   . . .   Nd5

White issued his 17th move and Black resigned (**1-0**).

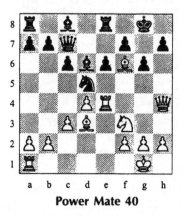

Power Mate 40

Q40: Do you see how White can make fast work of his
opponent?

POWER GAME **41**

Topalov vs. Bareev
Linares, 1994

White allows Black to equalize easily and then falls behind in development by wasting time. Black correctly opens the center with White's king still on its original square. To avoid trading queens, Black plays tactically, sacrificing both his rooks. This diverts White's queen out of play, and Black's remaining pieces (a queen, bishop, and knight) escort in the mate.

French Defense C11

1.	e4	e6
2.	d4	d5
3.	Nc3	Nf6
4.	Bg5	dxe4
5.	Nxe4	Be7
6.	Bxf6	Bxf6
7.	c3	...

Here, or on the next move, Ng1-f3 is more reliable.

7.	...	Nd7
8.	Qc2	e5
9.	dxe5	Nxe5
10.	f4	Ng6
11.	g3	0-0
12.	Bd3	Qd5!
13.	a3?	...

Preparing to castle queenside without losing the a-pawn. 13. Nxf6 + ? gxf6 14. 0-0-0 Qxh1 15. Be4 fails to the cross-pin 15. . . . Bf5. The best try would be 13. Ne2.

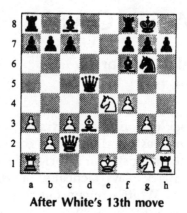

After White's 13th move

| 13. | ... | Nxf4! |
| 14. | Nxf6 + | ... |

White loses the exchange if 14. gxf4 by 14. . . . Bh4+ 15. Kf1 f5 16. Nd2 Qxh1.

14.	...	gxf6
15.	Bxh7 +	Kg7
16.	Qe4	...

After White's 16th move

| 16. | ... | Re8! |

A surprise pin preventing a queen trade. Black had other good moves: 16. . . . Qxe4+ 17. Bxe4 Re8; also 16. . . . Nd3+. But the text is more convincing.

| | 17. | Qxe8 | Bf5! |

A double-rook sacrifice, just like the old days.

| | 18. | Qxa8 | Qe4+ |

After Black's 18th move

| | 19. | Kf2 | ... |

Other king moves are no better:
(A) 19. Kf1 Qg2+ 20. Ke1 Nd3+ 21. Kd1 Bg4+.
(B) 19. Kd1 Qc2+ 20. Ke1 Nd3+.
(C) 19. Kd2 Qg2+! leads back into the game.

19.	...	Qg2+
20.	Ke3	Nd5+
21.	Kd4	Qd2+
22.	Kc5	Qe3+
23.	Kc4	...

If 23. Kxd5, then 23. . . . Be6#, a criss-cross mate; if 23. Kb5, then 23. . . . Qb6+ 24. Kc4 Ne3#.

| 23. | ... | Nb6+ |

White resigned (1-0).

Power Mate 41

Q41: Is there a sure mate in the offing?

POWER GAME *42*

Wilson vs. Saltzberg
New York, 1963

Black plays for unsound traps. He gains material, though his queen is lured out of position. White counters with a discovered check and deadly threats of his own. Black rushes his queen back to civilization for safety's sake, but winds up wasting more time and again relies too much on the queen, albeit in defense. But the defense fails, thanks to a check that causes pernicious interference. Black can choose how he gets mated.

King's Gambit Declined C30

1.	e4	e5
2.	f4	Bc5
3.	Nf3	....

Every King's Gambiteer knows the trap 3. fxe5? Qh4 + 4. g3 Qxe4 +, and Black picks up the h1-rook.

3.	....	Nc6?!

Correct and normal is 3. .... d6.

4.	fxe5	Nxe5?

After Black's 4th move

Black insists on offering material on e5, but this version of the trap is much better for White. Schlecter suggested 4. . . . d6, but that also favors White after 5. exd6 Qxd6 6. c3, followed by 7. d4.

5.	Nxe5!	Qh4 +
6.	g3	Qxe4 +
7.	Qe2	Qxh1

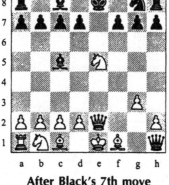

After Black's 7th move

Black has a rook, but there's no reason to be joyous.

8.	Ng6 +	Kd8?

This is a serious mistake. The only chance was 8. . . . Be7 9. Nxh8 Nf6, and eventually Black's king can slide over and pick up the knight in the corner.

9.	Nxh8	Qd5
10.	Bg2	. . .

Another way is 10. Nc3 Qf5 11. Bh3! Qf6 12. Nd5.

10.	. . .	Qf5

After Black's 10th move

11.	d4!	Bxd4

Loses instantly. As in an earlier variation, the best try was 11. . . . Be7, but after 12. Nc3, threatening 13. Bd5, White is still winning. For example, 12. . . . c6 13. Be4 Qf6 14. Bg5 Qe6 15. d5 cxd5 16. Bxd5 Qxe2+ 17. Kxe2 Bxg5 18. Nxf7+ and 19. Nxg5.

White now played his 12th move and Black resigned (**1-0**).

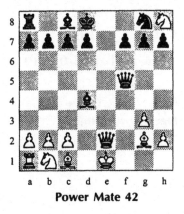

Power Mate 42

Q42: What unanticipated denouement did White concoct?

POWER GAME *43*

Murrey vs. Nikitinih
USSR, 1971

Proffering a pawn to open the f-file, White quickly mobilizes and steamrolls onward. Black, in turn, neglects development and relies too much on Her Ladyship. With such a military advantage, White can afford to sacrifice a couple of minor pieces to blow open the kingside. Unclothed and alone, the Black king is chased into the arena where the lions dine.

Falkbeer Counter Gambit C31

1.	e4	e5
2.	f4	d5
3.	exd5	e4
4.	d3	exd3?

This loses time, helping White to develop. Much better is 4. . . . Nf6.

5.	Bxd3	Qxd5

Keres-Lilienthal, Moscow, 1941 (1-0 in 19 moves) continued 5. . . . Nf6.

6.	Nc3	Qe6 +
7.	Nge2	Nh6

After Black's 7th move

A novelty, but 7. . . . Nf6 8. 0-0 Qb6+ 9. Kh1 Be7 10. Qe1 was unpleasant for Black (Keres-Vidmar, correspondence, 1936).

8.	**f5!**	. . .

Sacrificing a pawn to gain time, build development, and open lines for assault.

8.	. . .	Nxf5
9.	**0-0**	Ne3
10.	**Bxe3**	Qxe3 +
11.	**Kh1**	Bd6
12.	**Nf4!**	0-0

It's curtains for Black's queen after 12. . . . Bxf4? 13. Re1.

13.	**Qh5**	g6

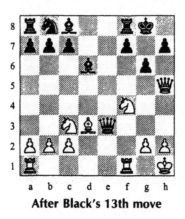

After Black's 13th move

After 13. . . . h6 White sustains the attack with 14. Rae1.

> **14.   Nxg6!   . . .**

White decides to break up Black's kingside pawns by unloading a bishop and knight, leaving Black without any pawn cover.

> **14.   . . .   fxg6**
> **15.   Bxg6!   hxg6**
> **16.   Qxg6 +   Kh8**
> **17.   Nd5   . . .**

After White's 17th move

17. ... Rxf1 +

Wicker gives 17. . . . Qe8 18. Rxf8 + Qxf8 19. Nf6 Bf5 20. Qxf5 Qh6 21. Qc8 + Bf8 (21. . . . Qf8 22. Qh3 + Kg7 23. Rf1 Qxf6 24. Rxf6 Kxf6 25. Qf3 + and 26. Qxb7) 22. Rf1!, and Black is completely tied up. White can always play 23. Qxb7 and 24. Qxa8.

18.	Rxf1	Qe2
19.	Qh6 +	Kg8
20.	Nf6 +	

Here Black resigned (1-0).

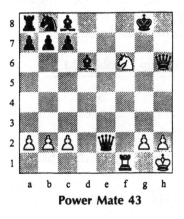

Power Mate 43

Q43: Can you work out the forced mate?

$\boldsymbol{P}$OWER GAME *44*

Lokasto vs. Marcinkowski
Poland, 1971

White plays a gambit line where he has to move the king out of check, giving up castling privileges. In turn, he gains a tempo on the black queen by developing a knight and establishes a classical pawn center. But after Black upholds his belligerent f4-pawn, White gets a little cavalier and incautiously assails Black's c5-bishop without preliminary reconnaissance. Black is ready with a sudden queen sac, which produces a criss-cross conclusion.

King's Bishop Gambit C33

1.	e4	e5
2.	f4	exf4
3.	Bc4	d5

Or 3. . . . Nf6, followed by d7-d5, obtaining a share of the center.

4.	Bxd5	Qh4 +

An ancient line, forcing White to move his hoary king. The modern move is 4. . . . Nf6.

5.	Kf1	Bd6

After Black's 5th move

A little-known suggestion by Svenonius. It seems no worse than the main line, 5. . . . g5.

6.	**Nf3**	**. . .**

The pawn offer 6. e5? doesn't work: 6. . . . Bxe5 7. Nf3 Qh5 8. Qe2 Nd7 9. d4; and now, 9. . . . Ne7 unpins the bishop.

6.	**. . .**	**Qh5**
7.	**d4**	**Ne7**
8.	**Nc3**	**f6**

Preparing to support the f4-pawn, so that White has difficulty getting his pieces out.

9.	**Qe1**	**. . .**

Something new. White unpins the f3-knight and strives directly to enforce e4-e5. The alternative was 9. Bc4, as in Szekely-Nylom, Abbazia, 1912.

9.	**. . .**	**Nc6**
10.	**Ne2**	**. . .**

Black has too many guys on e5, so White switches tactics to indirect methods. The text is designed to force g7-g5, blocking off the black queen's access to e5. On the other hand, the f4-pawn exerts a cramping influence over White's game.

| 10. | ... | g5 |

After Black's 10th move

| 11. | Bxc6 | ... |

Continuing with the same plan.

| 11. | ... | Nxc6 |

After Black's 11th move

| 12. | e5 | fxe5 |
| 13. | dxe5 | Bb4! |

Black is alert: after 13. . . . Nxe5? 14. Nxe5 Bxe5, White
has 15. Ng3!, along with 16. Qxe5+ and 17. Qxh8. The text
is better than an immediate 13. . . . Bc5 because then
White can slip in 14. Qc3.

| 14. | c3 | Bc5 |
| 15. | b4?? | . . . |

White is at a loss. Not knowing what to do, he walks into a
haymaker. Black played his 15th move and White resigned
(1-0).

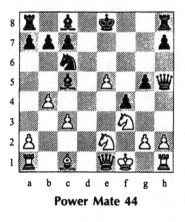

Power Mate 44

Q44: What shocker did Black play to end resistance?

POWER GAME 45

Stean vs. Corden
England, 1975

Employing the open lines in the center for attack, White gradually shifts his pieces over to the kingside. White's bishop reigns imperiously along the a2-g8 diagonal, but his opponent thinks it's tactically under his control. Overlooked, however, is White's breakthrough sacrifice on f6. This enables White to safely capture on g6 with check, exploiting the pin on f7. The shielding pawns are wiped away, and White's queen and bishop lead the procession to mate.

King's Gambit Accepted C33

1.	e4	e5
2.	f4	exf4
3.	Bc4	d5
4.	Bxd5	Nf6
5.	Nc3	Bb4
6.	Nf3	0-0

After Black's 6th move

The standard equalizing line for Black is 6. . . . Bxc3 7. dxc3
c6 8. Bc4 Qxd1+ 9. Kxd1 Nxe4 10. Bxf4 0-0. The text is
not an improvement.

	7.	0-0	Bxc3

This gives White the two bishops, generally advantageous
in open positions.

	8.	dxc3	c6
	9.	Bb3	Qb6+
	10.	Kh1	Nxe4
	11.	Qe1	Bf5
	12.	Nh4	Re8
	13.	Bxf4	Nf6
	14.	Qg3	Bg6

After Black's 14th move

On 14. . . . Ne4, White has 15. Qf3 Bg6 16. Nxg6 hxg6 17.
Bxf7+ Kxf7 18. Bc7+, which is harmful to the black queen.

	15.	Nxg6	hxg6
	16.	Bxb8	Raxb8

After Black's 16th move

17.	Rxf6!	gxf6
18.	Qxg6+	...

A bolt from the white, set up by the previous three moves, taking advantage of the pin on the f7-pawn. Black is helpless against the combined attack of queen and bishop.

18.	...	Kh8
19.	Bxf7	Qe3

Played to stop 20. Qh6#. Black's queen tries to get back to the critical area, but it's too late.

20.	Qxf6+	Kh7

White displayed his 21st move and Black resigned (1-0).

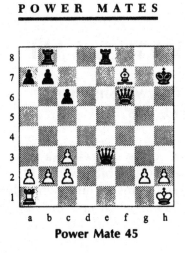

Power Mate 45

Q45: What move ushered in an era of forced mate?

Levin vs. W. Shipman
Concord, 1995

By failing to advance the d-pawn in a timely way, White is unable to capture the gambit pawn at f4, which is turned into a battering ram against White's kingside. Together with pressure from Black's queen and bishop, White has little choice but to weaken his kingside. Black's queen invades, and so does his knight, and there's a knight mate ending with a partial smothering.

King's Gambit Accepted C39

1.	e4	e5
2.	f4	exf4
3.	Nf3	g5
4.	h4	g4
5.	Ne5	d6
6.	Nxg4	Be7
7.	Bc4?	. . .

After White's 7th move

A mistake. The advance of the d-pawn was indicated. A standard line is 7. d4 Bxh4+ 8. Nf2 Qg5 9. Qf3 Nc6 10. Qxf4 Bxf2+ 11. Kxf2 Qxf4+ 12. Bxf4 Nxd4, and despite Black's extra pawn, the chances are rated about even.

7.	...	Bxh4+
8.	Nf2	Qg5
9.	Qf3	...

It's too late to correct the error. If 9. d4, then 9. . . . Nf6 10. Qf3 Ng4 gains material.

9.	...	Nc6!
10.	0-0?	...

After White's 10th move

This makes things too easy. The only chance to wage war was 10. d4, deflecting the knight from e5. After 10. . . . Nxd4 11. Qxf4 Bxf2+ 12. Kxf2 Qxf4+ 13. Bxf4 Nxc2, Black wins the exchange, but White can muddy the waters with 14. Nc3 Nxa1 15. Nd5.

10.	...	Ne5
11.	Qb3	f3

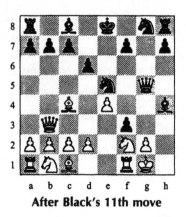

After Black's 11th move

Threatens mate on the move.

	12.	Bxf7 +	. . .

An immediate 12. g4 gives Black the option of 12. . . . Bxg4 13. d4 Qg6 14. Kh2 Be6 15. Rg1 Bxf2 16. Rxg6 hxg6+ 17. Bh6 Rxh6#.

	12.	. . .	Ke7!

White was hoping for 12. . . . Nxf7 13. Qxf3, but the knight will not be distracted.

	13.	g4	. . .

Forced. But now come three dreaded creeping moves with the queen as she inches her way in.

	13.	. . .	Qf4
	14.	Kh1	Qg3
	15.	Rg1	Qxf2
	16.	d4	. . .

Ten moves too late.

	16.	. . .	Nxg4
	17.	Bf4	. . .

Black now forced mate on his 18th move (1-0).

Power Mate 46

Q46: How does Black put an end to all this?

Van Mil vs. Reinderman
Wijk Sonnevanek, 1993

Black falls behind in development, costing him a pawn. White, with the initiative, beachheads at h6. To avoid a trade of bishops, Black withdraws his bishop to h8. After White's pieces deploy to more effective points, Black, failing to appreciate White's hold over the h6-f8 diagonal, trips into a losing deflection.

Philidor Defense C41

1.	e4	e5
2.	Nf3	d6
3.	d4	exd4
4.	Nxd4	g6

Larsen's ambitious fianchetto. Safe and passive is Antoshin's Bf8-e7.

5.	Nc3	Bg7
6.	Be3	Nf6
7.	Qd2	0-0
8.	0-0-0	. . .

The players castle on opposite sides. Whose attack will get there first?

8.	. . .	Re8
9.	f3	. . .

White sets up exactly as in the Yugoslav Dragon. This last move solidifies the center and prevents Nf6-g4, annoying the e3-bishop. Next on the agenda is the advance of the g- and h-pawns, so Black creates a diversion in the center.

9.	. . .	d5

After Black's 9th move

Essentially a sacrifice, since the d-pawn is untenable on this square.

10.	Nb3	c6
11.	Bh6	Bh8

Retaining his king's bishop but abandoning the f8-h6 diagonal.

12.	exd5	cxd5
13.	Nxd5	...

White captures the free pawn. Why not?

13		Nc6
14	Nc3	Qb6
15	Bc4	Ne5

After Black's 15th move

Black has some activity, but not enough to compensate for the pawn minus.

	16.	Bb5	Bd7
	17.	Bxd7	Nfxd7

After Black's 17th move

Better is 17. . . . Nexd7. The text turns over the d5-square, of which White's knight soon makes good use.

	18.	Rhe1	Nf8
	19.	Nd5	Qa6
	20.	Kb1	Rac8

To prevent 21. Nc7.

	21.	Qb4	Qc6?

Hoping for 22. Ne7 + ? Rxe7 23. Qxe7 Qxc2 + 24. Ka1 Nd3, and Black wins. But it is a case of the wrong piece going to the right square. The only move was 21. . . . Nc6. White now forced mate on his 23rd move (**1–0**).

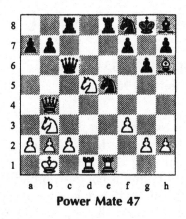

Power Mate 47

Q47: What did Black's last move miss?

POWER GAME *48*

Astapovich vs. Golosov
Novosibirsk, 1967

Black develops passively with Bf8-e7 and allows White's knight to sit on f5 unnoticed. Furthermore, he weakens f7 by precipitously moving the castled rook. His shoddy play is compounded by taking a booby-trapped pawn on e4. So White sacrifices a bishop, drawing out and exposing the king and finessing with a move that finishes. It's over before it really begins.

Scotch Game C47

1.	e4	e5
2.	Nf3	Nc6
3.	d4	exd4
4.	Nxd4	Nf6
5.	Nc3	. . .

Mieses's idea, 5. Nxc6 bxc6 6. e5, is all the rage these days. This system isn't bad either.

5.	. . .	Be7

After Black's 5th move

Standard is 5. . . . Bb4, and recently 5. . . . Bc5 has had attention. The text is terribly passive.

6. Nf5 ...

White can get a clear advantage with 6. Nxc6 bxc6 (or 6. . . . dxc6 7. Qxd8 +) 7. e5. The move played, which tries to avoid exchanges, is somewhat risky. The undermining move d7-d5 is in the air, so White must be circumspect.

6. ... 0-0

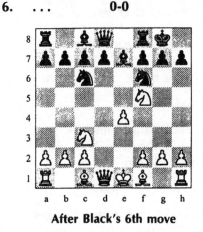

After Black's 6th move

Here 6. . . . d5 probably doesn't work: 7. Nxg7 + Kf8 8. Bh6, and though Black can avert mate, it's not clear how his rook gets out of the corner.

7. Bg5 Re8

Black is trying to set up a shot on the e-file, while White remains uncastled. But this rook move leaves f7 susceptible to a combination. If Black did not want to venture forth with 7. . . . d5!?, then he should have played 7. . . . d6, creating a cramped but steady position.

8. Bc4 Nxe4?

After Black's 8th move

Black's shot, but it's a blank. The e-pawn is baited.

9.   Bxf7+!   ...

Going for the gold. It would also be possible to settle for the gain of a piece: 9. Nxe7+ Nxe7 10. Nxe4 d5 11. Bb3 dxe4 12. Qxd8 Rxd8 13. Bxe7.

9.   ...   Kxf7

Not taking back is also in the bad category (see Aristotle's theory of classes). White's sacrifice exposes Black's king to attack.

10.   Qd5+   Kf8

On 10. . . . Kg6, there ensues 11. Nh4+ Kh5 12. g4+ Kxg4 13. Rg1+ Kh5 14. Qf7+ g6 15. Qxh7#, another horror story. White now played his 11th move and Black didn't feel the need to continue (**1-0**).

Power Mate 48

Q48: What subtle intrusion did White play to set up mate?

POWER GAME **49**

Banas vs. Lukacs
Trnava, 1986

White takes a pawn on e5, but it costs him time, and he discombobulates his own forces in retreat. Black sees his opportunity, and sacrifices a knight on f3 to shatter White's kingside. Black's queen immediately heads for the holes created near the enemy king, and White tries to defend, but his disarrayed pieces are ill-equipped for the job. Mate follows at h2 or g2.

Four Knights Game C48

1.	e4	e5
2.	Nf3	Nc6
3.	Nc3	Nf6
4.	Bb5	Nd4
5.	Ba4	Bc5
6.	0-0	0-0
7.	Nxe5?	. . .

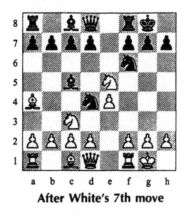

After White's 7th move

This is a mistake. If White wanted to grab the e5-pawn, he should have done it before castling. Safer was 7. d3, preparing to bring out the c1-bishop.

| 7. | ... | d6 |
| 8. | Nc4 | ... |

Developing the knight to f3 allows the pin 8. . . . Bg4, leading to a disruptive exchange on f3 and the annihilation of White's kingside cover.

| 8. | ... | Bg4 |

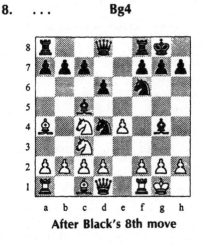

After Black's 8th move

Even without the pin, this move is strong, for Black gains control of the f3-square.

| 9. | Qe1 | ... |

After White's 9th move

White couldn't respond with 9. f3 because of the demolishing double check, 9. . . . Nxf3+.

| 9. | ... | Nf3+ |

This sacrifice was suggested ages ago by Alekhine, who concluded that Black would have a strong attack, ages and ages hence.

| 10. | gxf3 | Bxf3 |
| 11. | d4 | ... |

With 11. h3, White runs into the steamrolling 11. . . . Ng4 12. hxg4 Qh4 and 13. . . . Qh1#.

| 11. | ... | Qc8 |

Ignoring the attack on his bishop, Black heads for the king.

| 12. | Ne3 | Qh3 |
| 13. | dxc5 | |

Black played his 13th move and White resigned (1-0).

Power Mate 49

Q49: How did Black force White's resignation?

*P*OWER GAME *50*

Felber vs. Crawford
New York, 1993

Black cedes the initiative in order to inflict doubled pawns on both sides of the board. Unfortunately, these transactions actually increase White's dynamism, opening the a- and f-files for rook activity. White exploits the open lines further by shifting his queen to the kingside, and at the critical juncture, finds a breakthrough sacrifice at f7. A white rook rides the A-train to the seventh rank and arrives in time for mate.

Giuoco Piano C50

1.	e4	e5
2.	Bc4	Bc5
3.	Nf3	Nc6
4.	0-0	Nf6
5.	d3	d6
6.	Be3	Bxe3
7.	fxe3	Na5
8.	Bb3	Nxb3

After Black's 8th move

Black's 6th and 8th moves are played to give White doubled pawns, but the recaptures actually strengthen White's game by giving him open a- and f-files.

9.	axb3	0-0
10.	Nc3	Re8

It's better to keep the rook on f8, until White's pressure on the half-open f-file is completely neutralized. Steinitz and Chigorin used to play Nf6-g4 and Ng4-h6 here and then advance the f-pawn. When Black eventually comes around to this maneuver in this game, it's too late.

11.	Qe1	...

This is a typical way for White's queen to sidle into the game. Later it will transfer to h4, gearing for kingside activity.

11.	...	Qe7
12.	Nh4	g6
13.	Nf3	c6

After Black's 13th move

14.	Qh4	Kg7
15.	Rae1	...

Intending 16. Re2 and 17. Ref2, turning up the heat on the f-file.

15.   ...   Ng4?

The knight is going to have to move sooner or later, but
better would be 15. . . . h6 and 16. . . . Ng8.

16.   Ng5   Nh6

After Black's 16th move

17.   Rxf7 + !   Nxf7
18.   Qxh7 +   Kf8

On 18. . . . Kf6 there follows 19. Rf1 + Kxg5 (19. . . . Bf5
is met by 20. exf5) 20. Rxf7 Qe6 (20. . . . Qd8 21. h4 + Kg4
22. Qxg6 + Kxh4 23. Rh7#) 21. h4 + Kg4 22. Qh6! Qxf7
23. Qg5#.

19.   Rf1   Bf5

Black tries to thwart the attack, but the damage has been
done.

20.   exf5   Qxg5
21.   fxg6   Ke7

White played his 22nd and 23rd moves, and Black resigned
(1-0).

Power Mate 50

Q50: How did White end this game in mate?

POWER GAME **51**

Waterman vs. Samo
San Francisco, 1974

Obtaining a spatial advantage by advancing pawns, White thwarts enemy development and keeps his opponent cramped. Black tries to alleviate his condition by exchanges, but they only encourage White's war-waging. A bishop is sacrificed, the a-file is opened against Black's king, and an unbelievable queen offering prevents escape. This becomes mate in any language or any earthly place.

Ruy Lopez C65

1.	e4	e5
2.	Nf3	Nc6
3.	Bb5	Nf6
4.	Qe2	d6
5.	d4	Bd7
6.	Bxc6	Bxc6
7.	Nc3	Qe7

After Black's 7th move

Leads to congestion in the ranks. Simpler is 7. . . . exd4 8.
Nxd4, followed by Bf8-e7 and kingside castling.

| 8. | 0-0! | 0-0-0 |

Black drops a piece in the line 8. . . . exd4 9. Nxd4 Bxe4?
10. Nxe4 Nxe4 11. Re1.

| 9. | d5! | . . . |

This advance keeps his opponent greatly constricted, with
Black unable to complete his development satisfactorily.

9.	. . .	Bd7
10.	a4	g6
11.	Be3	Kb8

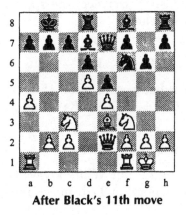

After Black's 11th move

Black moves his king over to guard against potential queenside invasions. In the end, it doesn't work.

| 12. | Qc4 | Ng4? |

This helps propel the bishop into the attack. The knight
should have remained on f6.

| 13. | Nb5 | Bxb5 |

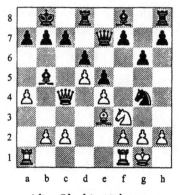

After Black's 13th move

| 14. | Bxa7+! | . . . |

A kind of classic bishop sacrifice, the specific idea being to open the a-file with check.

| 14. | . . . | Kxa7 |
| 15. | axb5+ | Kb8 |

Black runs into a body slam after 15. . . . Kb6?, via 16. Ra6+! bxa6 17. Qc6+ Ka7 18. Ra1, followed by Rxa6 and Ra6-a8#.

| 16. | Ra3 | Kc8 |

Trying to escape to d7, but White knows how to stop that. He played his unbelievable 17th move and Black resigned (1-0).

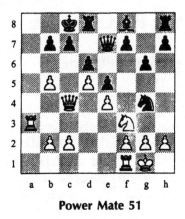

Power Mate 51

Q51: What extraordinary move by White barred Black's escape and set up a mate?

POWER GAME **52**

Kupreicik vs. Planinc
Sombor, 1970

White establishes a classical pawn center, and just when Black thinks he's neutralized it, he walks into a bristling bishop sacrifice at f7. His king must flee toward the wing, but a processional of White's pieces head toward the gloomy gravesite. A pall hangs over the mated Black king.

Ruy Lopez C66

1.	e4	e5
2.	Nf3	Nc6
3.	Bb5	Be7
4.	0-0	Nf6
5.	Re1	d6
6.	c3	0-0
7.	d4	Bd7
8.	h3	. . .

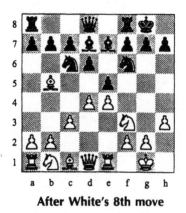

After White's 8th move

A waiting move. If 8. Nbd2, then 8. . . . Nxd4 9. Nxd4?
(better 9. cxd4) 9. . . . exd4 10. Bxd7 dxc3, winning a pawn.

| 8. | ... | Re8 |
| 9. | Nbd2 | ... |

Now this is okay. The line given in the previous note no
longer works for Black with his rook occupying e8.

9.	...	Bf8
10.	Bc4!?	exd4
11.	cxd4	d5

Looking forward to 12. exd5 Rxe1+ 13. Qxe1 Nb4, regaining the pawn with advantage.

| 12. | Bb3! | dxe4 |

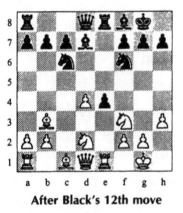

After Black's 12th move

This opens the a2-g8 diagonal, allowing a combination.

| 13. | Bxf7+!? | ... |

Why not? If 13. Ng5, Black can defend himself with
13. . . . Be6.

| 13. | ... | Kxf7 |
| 14. | Qb3+ | Kg6? |

This loses. There is a way out, however, with 14. . . . Be6!
15. Ng5+ Kg8 16. Nxe6 Na5! 17. Nxd8+ Nxb3 18. axb3
Rexd8 19. Nxe4 Rxd4.

| 15. | Nh4+ | Kh5 |

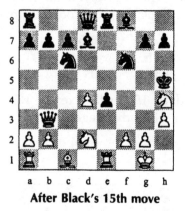

After Black's 15th move

| 16. | Nxe4! | . . . |

Threatens 17. Qf3+.

| 16. | . . . | Rxe4 |

If 16. . . . Nxe4, then 17. Qf3+ Kxh4 18. Rxe4+ Rxe4 19.
Qxe4+ Kh5 20. Qxh7# becomes a reality.

| 17. | Rxe4 | g5 |

Hoping to hide behind the g-pawn, but that's no place to
hide.

| 18. | Qf7+ | Kh6 |

White now played his 19th move and Black resigned (1-0).

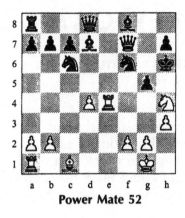

Power Mate 52

Q52: How did White force mate from this position?

Brynell vs. Almasi
Malmö, 1994

White develops rather planlessly, and Black has no trouble equalizing. Eventually, White's ideas get nowhere, and Black mounts a kingside attack. Out of the blue comes a knight sacrifice on f3, and Black busts up White's kingside. One more sac, a deflecting bishop shot, puts White away for good.

Ruy Lopez C68

1.	e4	e5
2.	Nf3	Nc6
3.	Bb5	a6
4.	Bxc6	dxc6
5.	0-0	Qd6
6.	Na3	Be6
7.	Qe2	f6
8.	Rd1	0-0-0
9.	d4	Bg4

The pin is created to pressure White's center.

10.	Be3	Qe6
11.	Nc4	exd4
12.	Bxd4	Ne7
13.	Be3?!	. . .

After White's 13th move

An interesting struggle is taking shape, but here White commits an inexactitude. Better was 13. Bc3, keeping an eye on the e5-square while leaving e3 vacant. This would enable White's queen to threaten 14. Qe3 and 15. Qa7.

	13.	...	Re8!

The e4-pawn is poisoned: 13. . . . Rxd1+ 14. Rxd1 Qxe4? 15. Nb6+! cxb6 16. Bxb6!, with mate or win of the queen to ensue.

	14.	Ncd2	f5
	15.	Re1	Ng6

If 15. . . . fxe4, White has 16. Ng5 Qf5 17. Qc4.

	16.	exf5	Qxf5
	17.	Qc4	Bd6

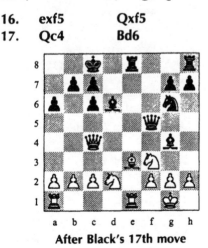

After Black's 17th move

Black is catching up in development, forebodingly gathering his pieces in the sector of White's king.

| | 18. | Nd4 | . . . |

Another slip. The knight is heading to the wrong part of the board. Better is 18. h3 Bxf3 19. Nxf3, eliminating one of the dangerous black bishops.

| | 18. | . . . | Qh5 |
| | 19. | Nf1? | . . . |

This was the last chance for h2-h3.

| | 19. | . . . | c5! |

Shunting the knight off to the queenside.

| | 20. | Nb3 | Ne5 |

A clear sign that White has lost the battle. Black's forces move in at will.

| | 21. | Qc3 | . . . |

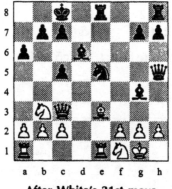

After White's 21st move

| | 21. | . . . | Nf3 + ! |
| | 22. | gxf3 | Bxf3 |

Threatens 23. . . . Qh3 and 24. . . . Qg2#.

23.   Nbd2

Black now played his 23rd move and White resigned (**1-0**).

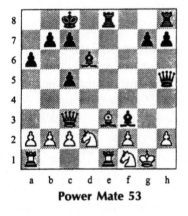

Power Mate 53

Q53: What stunning move did White overlook?

POWER GAME **54**

Kumaran vs. Miles
Dublin, 1993

Black's plan is one-dimensional: to develop and castle queen-side expeditiously. But the queenside turns out to be a hornet's nest, and White's queen and minor pieces prove to be a terrific assault force. It takes no time for White's coordinated firepower to check and menace Black's king into oblivion.

Queen-Pawn Game D02

1.	**d4**	**Nc6**

Miles plays offbeat openings. The text allows transposition to the Nimzovich Defense, 2. e4, and is indicative of plans that attack the center with pieces instead of pawns.

2.	**Nf3**	**d5**

Inviting 3. c4, transposing into a Chigorin's Queen's Gambit, which Miles has also tried.

3.	**g3**	**Bg4**
4.	**Bg2**	**Qd7**
5.	**c4**	. . .

The book moves here are 5. 0-0 and 5. h3.

5.	**. . .**	**e6**

Reinforcing the center. Certainly 5. . . . dxc4 is worth a look, but 6. d5 Nb4? 7. Ne5 Qf5 8. Qa4+ Kd8 9. Nxf7+ Qxf7 10. Qxb4 conveys a winning impression for White.

6.	**0-0**	**0-0-0**
7.	**Nc3**	**dxc4**
8.	**Qa4**	**Bb4?**

After Black's 8th move

This loses by force. Black might be able to survive with
8. . . . Bxf3 9. Bxf3 Nge7, but White's in command. Now
the f3-knight lives to inflict deflective damage.

    9.   Ne5!   **Nxe5**

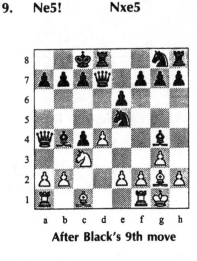

After Black's 9th move

    10.   Qxa7!   **. . .**

A deadly zwischenzug. White now threatens mate at a8.

    10.   . . .   **c6**

The king needs an escape hatch (10. . . . Nc6 11. Qa8+
Nb8 12. Qxb7#).

      11.   Bf4   Bd6

If 11. . . . Qc7, White is ahead after 12. Bxe5 Bd6 13. Bxg7;
and 11. . . . Qxd4 12. Qxd4 Rxd4 13. Bxe5 is good for
White too.

      12.   Qa8+   Kc7

After Black's 12th move

On 12. . . . Bb8, White can play 13. Bxe5.

      13.   Nb5+!   Kb6

Capturing 13. . . . cxb5 permits 14. Qxb7#. White now
played two more moves and Black resigned on his 15th move
(1-0).

Power Mate 54

Q54: How can White force mate?

*P*OWER GAME *55*

Baburin vs. Adianto
Liechtenstein, 1993

Some nice maneuvering occurs here, but much of it favors
Black, and White weakens himself and lags in development.
Suddenly, Black launches a kingside attack by advancing the
h-pawn, leading to an invasive knight sacrifice on g3. Black
follows with an aggressive king move, clearing his own home
rank, and setting up a spectacular sacrificial orgy. Naturally,
White is mated.

Queen's Gambit Accepted D25

1.	d4	d5
2.	c4	dxc4
3.	Nf3	Nf6
4.	e3	a6
5.	Bxc4	b5
6.	Bd3	Bb7

After Black's 6th move

Normally Black plays e7-e6, followed by c7-c5, and then a7-
a6, followed by b7-b5. Here, Black reverses the sequence,
perhaps hoping to confuse his opponent.

7.	0-0	e6
8.	a4	b4
9.	Nbd2	Nbd7
10.	Nb3	c5
11.	dxc5	Nxc5
12.	Nxc5	Bxc5
13.	Qc2	Rc8
14.	Qe2	Qb6
15.	e4	h6
16.	a5	Qa7

After Black's 16th move

White has played well up to here. He should continue with
17. Bf4, building his game.

17.	Nd2	. . .

The start of a bad plan. Over the next three moves White
loses ground, weakening his king's position in the process.

17.	. . .	Qa8

18.	Kh1	h5
19.	f3	h4
20.	Nc4	Nh5
21.	Be3	...

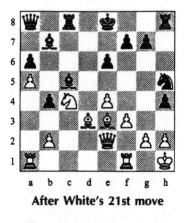

After White's 21st move

| 21. | ... | Ng3 + ! |

Beginning a decisive mating attack. White is now forced to capture, opening the h-file with check.

| 22. | hxg3 | hxg3 + |
| 23. | Kg1 | Ke7!! |

A bold move that clears the back rank for the heavy pieces. Paradoxically, sometimes the center is the king's safest place.

| 24. | Qe1 | ... |

Black now played his 24th move and White resigned (0-1).

Power Mate 55

Q55: Can you formulate Black's forced mate?

Vera vs. Garcia
Matanzas, 1992

The fight begins when the players castle on opposite sides, and White supersedes by calling the kingside pawns to arms first. The h-file is opened, with White pressing ahead, but Black counters with a gain of White's queen. It's a trick, however, and White wins without a queen, thanks to his queen-rook and mobile knights. They hop right into mate.

Queen's Gambit Declined D37

1.	d4	d5
2.	c4	e6
3.	Nc3	Nf6
4.	Nf3	Be7
5.	Bf4	0-0
6.	e3	c5

In this symmetrical center, White maintains the edge by virtue of going first.

7.	dxc5	Bxc5
8.	Qc2	Nc6
9.	a3	Qa5
10.	0-0-0	. . .

By castling on the opposite wing, White signals his intention of beginning full scale-combat. Pawn storms are in the offing.

10.	. . .	Bd7
11.	g4	. . .

After White's 11th move

This once-fashionable move has in recent years been replaced by 11. Kb1, as well as 11. cxd5.

| 11. | ... | Rfc8 |

White has a dangerous initiative after 11. . . . Nxg4 12. Rg1.

| 12. | Kb1 | Bf8 |

This was Black's choice in Gelfand-Belyavsky, Linares, 1990. A year later, also at Linares and against the same opponent, Belyavsky introduced his improvement 12. . . . b5!!, and this move more or less put 11. g4 to sleep.

| 13. | Ng5 | g6 |
| 14. | h4 | ... |

White begins his inexorable line-opening advances on the kingside. The plan is to clear the h-file for major pieces.

14.	...	Bg7
15.	h5	Be8
16.	hxg6	hxg6
17.	f3!	...

After White's 17th move

Not played so much to protect the g4-pawn as to allow the queen to cross to h2.

> **17.   ...   b5?**

The action on the queenside turns out to be slow. Vera indicates 17. . . . e5!, a preemptive strike in the center, is the better course of play. A likely line is then: 18. Bg3 d4 19. exd4 Nxd4 20. Qh2 Bc6 21. Bxe5 Nxf3 22. Nxf3 Bxf3 23. Nd5 Bxd5 24. cxd5.

> **18.   cxb5   ...**

But not 18. cxd5? because of 18. . . . b4.

> **18.   ...   Ne7**
> **19.   Be5   d4**

If 19. . . . a6, to clear more queenside lines, White has just enough time to break in on the kingside: 20. Qh2 axb5 21. Be2 b4 22. Qh8 + !! Bxh8 23. Rxh8 + Kxh8 24. Bxf6 + Kg8 25. Rh1 Kf8 26. Rh8 + Ng8 27. Nh7#.

> **20.   Bxd4   Ned5**

After Black's 20th move

Or 20. . . . Nfd5 21. Qh2 Nxc3+ 22. bxc3 f6 23. Qh7+ Kf8 24. Bxf6! Bxf6 25. Nxe6#.

21.   Nxd5!   . . .

A queen sacrifice! What's this all about?

21.   . . .   Rxc2

On 21. . . . Nxd5, White wins by 22. Qh2, doubling on the h-file.

22.   Nxf6+   Kf8

If Black takes back, 22. . . . Bxf6, then 23. Bxf6 insures a back-rank corner mate.

23.   Ngh7+   Ke7

In this tense position, White played his 24th move and Black resigned (**1-0**).

Power Mate 56

Q56: Can you work out White's forced mate?

Ehlvest vs. Martinovsky
Linares, 1994

This is a linear plot all the way. White telegraphs his plan to invade along the b1-h7 diagonal, and Black cooperates with the occupied force by voluntarily shifting his army to the queenside. White even offers a rook to distract the enemy queen. Once White deduces how to prevent escape at e7, the conclusion becomes axiomatic. If you're outplayed, you get mated.

Queen's Gambit Declined D37

1.	d4	Nf6
2.	Nf3	d5
3.	c4	e6
4.	Nc3	Be7
5.	Bf4	0-0
6.	e3	c5
7.	dxc5	Bxc5
8.	cxd5	. . .

After White's 8th move

Usually, White looks for an edge with 8. Qc2.

8.	...	Nxd5
9.	Nxd5	exd5
10.	a3	Nc6
11.	Bd3	...

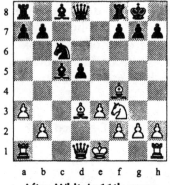

8
7
6
5
4
3
2
1

a b c d e f g h

After White's 11th move

Threatens 11. Bxh7+ Kxh7 12. Qc2+ and 13. Qxc5, winning a pawn.

| 11. | ... | h6? |

A severe weakness and a known error. Better would be 11. . . . Bd6 or 11. . . . Bb6, backing off the exposed bishop.

| 12. | Bb1 | Re8 |

White's intentions are clear: Qd1-c2 and Qc2-h7#. The text gives Black's king a fleeing square.

| 13. | Qc2 | ... |

Why does Black's kingside seem so defenseless? Because there's no knight at f6.

| 13. | ... | Qa5+ |

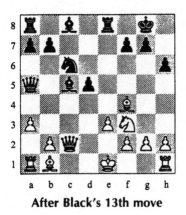

After Black's 13th move

| 14. | b4! | Bxb4+ |

If 14. . . . Nxb4, then 15. Qh7+ Kf8 16. 0-0, and White is ready to pick up the g7-pawn, with continuing attack.

| 15. | axb4 | . . . |

White takes the bishop, even though he thereby sacrifices his rook, because he wants to destroy Black's control of the a3-f8 diagonal.

| 15. | . . . | Qxa1 |

White played his 16th move and Black resigned (**1-0**).

Power Mate 57

Q57: Does White have a forcible mate?

$\boldsymbol{P}$OWER GAME $\boldsymbol{58}$

Kasparov vs. Larsen
Brussels, 1987

White accepts an isolated d-pawn, but with insistent development and centralization converts it into a space edge and concomitant attack. When the d4-d5 break occurs, Black has fallen into a forced retreat. White turns his attention to the kingside, which is devoid of its praetorian guard, now mainly on the queenside. Using the a2-bishop as his attacking pivot, White sacrifices his queen so that his minor pieces can put an end to the resistance—a victory of the underlings.

Queen's Gambit Declined D40

1.	Nf3	Nf6
2.	c4	c5
3.	Nc3	Nc6
4.	e3	e6
5.	d4	d5
6.	a3	cxd4
7.	exd4	Be7
8.	Bd3	. . .

The alternative is 8. c5, establishing a queenside pawn majority. With the text, White invites Black into a Queen's Gambit Accepted.

8.	. . .	0-0
9.	0-0	dxc4
10.	Bxc4	b6

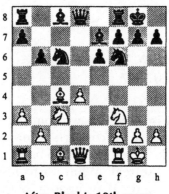

After Black's 10th move

Or 10. . . . a6 and 11. . . . b5. In any case, a typical isolated queen-pawn position has arisen. White has more operating space and the initiative.

	11.	**Qd3**	. . .

Not immediately 11. Ba2 because of 11. . . . Ba6!, cutting across White's plans.

11.	**. . .**	**Bb7**
12.	**Ba2**	**Qd6**
13.	**Bg5**	**Rfd8**
14.	**Rad1**	**Nh5**

Seeking the exchange of bishops, which White evades by retreating to the home rank.

15.	**Bc1**	**Nf4**

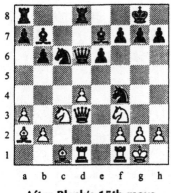

After Black's 15th move

	16.	Qe4	Ng6

An unusual square for Black's king-knight. It knocks out any mating ideas with Ba2-b1 and Qe4xh7, but it does not deter d4-d5 or a later Qh5. White may someday use the center to transfer to the kingside.

17.	Rfe1	Bf8
18.	Qe2	. . .

Setting up the advance of the d-pawn. Playing 18. d5 would have run into 18. . . . Ne7.

18.	. . .	Rac8

The sequel shows that there is no time for this move. Larsen might have tried 18. . . . Nf4.

19.	d5!	. . .

White converts his spatial lead into greater initiative.

19.	. . .	exd5
20.	Nxd5	Qb8

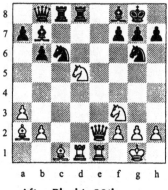

After Black's 20th move

	21.	Ng5!	. . .

Suddenly, all of White's pieces are pointed in the direction of Black's king, and most of Black's army is on the other side of the board.

21.	. . .	Re8
22.	Qh5	Rxe1 +
23.	Rxe1	h6

White played his 24th move and Black resigned (**1-0**).

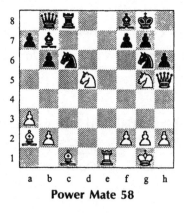

Power Mate 58

Q58: How did White punctuate this modern-day masterpiece?

POWER GAME 59

Kramnik vs. Ehlvest
Riga, 1995

Play rages on both flanks, with each side taking chances characteristic of the opening, though White pushes a little faster and manages to open the center to his advantage. He castles queenside, into a potential attack himself, but his dominance tells along the middle rows. Black's king is caught in the midsection, and he's flattened by the one-two of a queen and rook.

Queen's Gambit Declined D44

1.	Nf3	d5
2.	d4	Nf6
3.	c4	c6
4.	Nc3	e6
5.	Bg5	dxc4
6.	e4	b5
7.	e5	h6
8.	Bh4	g5
9.	Nxg5	hxg5
10.	Bxg5	Nbd7

After Black's 10th move

The ultra-sharp Botvinnik Variation. Practically every tournament brings new lines and improvements to theory. Activity sweeps the entire board.

| 11. | g3 | ... |

Preparing Bf1-g2. The bishop works best on the long diagonal.

| 11. | ... | Qa5 |
| 12. | exf6 | Ba6 |

Cutting across White's plan. After 13. Bg2 b4, White can no longer castle kingside. Kramnik adjusts.

| 13. | Qf3 | Rc8? |

Guarding and also unpinning the c6-pawn while preparing c6-c5. In retrospect, the move looks too slow, and the sharp b5-b4 would be in order.

| 14. | Be2 | b4 |
| 15. | Ne4 | c5 |

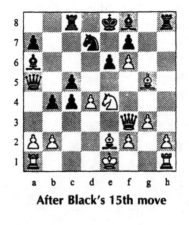

After Black's 15th move

| 16. | d5! | ... |

First suggested by I. Sokolov, this thrust ensures the opening of the center.

16.	. . .	exd5
17.	Qf5!	dxe4
18.	0-0-0	. . .

Castling queenside to seize the d-file and foster the attack.

18.	. . .	Rc7
19.	Bg4	. . .

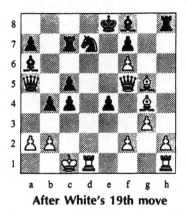

After White's 19th move

19.	. . .	Bb5

Black has to defend d7. Kramnik gives a long variation to show that counterattack with 19. . . . Qxa2 fails to 20. Rxd7 Qa1+ 21. Kd2 Qxb2+ 22. Ke3 Qd4+ 23. Rxd4 cxd4+ 24. Kxd4 Bc5+ 25. Qxc5 Rxc5 26. Kxc5 b3 27. Kb4 Rg8 28. h4, and White is winning.

20.	Qxe4+	Kd8
21.	Bxd7	Bxd7

After 21. . . . Rxd7, Kramnik intended 22. Bf4!, threatening 23. Qa8#.

22.	Rhe1	Bh6
23.	Qa8+	. . .

Shifting the attack from the center to the back rank.

| 23. | ... | Rc8 |
| 24. | Rxd7+ | Kxd7 |

With the black king exposed to the cruel elements, Ehlvest resigned after White played his 25th move (1-0).

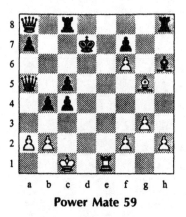

Power Mate 59

Q59: With what winning line does White conclude?

POWER GAME 60

Piket vs. Sturna
Debrecen, 1992

It's a humble, yet moral tale, more like a treatment than a script. White violates the principle of development, engaging in hand-to-hand fighting without enough buildup. White's supplies are insufficient, and his king is trapped in the center. Black sacrifices his queen to gain time for invading rooks and minor pieces, and for White the third act ends tragically. Good chess, good theater.

Queen's Gambit Declined D55

1.	d4	d5
2.	c4	e6
3.	Nc3	Be7
4.	Nf3	Nf6
5.	Bg5	h6
6.	Bxf6	Bxf6
7.	e3	0-0
8.	Qc2	Na6

After Black's 8th move

Introduced by Kasparov in his 1985 World Championship Match with Karpov (fourth game). The idea is c7-c5, and if d4xc5, then Na6xc5.

9.	Rd1	c5
10.	dxc5	Qa5
11.	cxd5	Nxc5
12.	Nd4	. . .

Black gets a lead in development with 12. dxe6 Bxe6. In that fourth match game, Karpov played it ultra-safe with 12. Qd2 Rd8 13. Nd4, eventually winning.

12.	. . .	exd5
13.	a3	Ne6!

This is the surest way to equality—going after White's best-placed piece, the d4-knight.

14.	Ndb5?	. . .

Too ambitious. Preparing to castle by 14. Be2 would be much safer.

14.	. . .	a6
15.	b4	Qd8
16.	Rxd5	Bd7!

After Black's 16th move

A simple move of deceptive strength. White might have been hoping for 16. . . . Qb6?? 17. Rd6 or 16. . . . Qe8 (or 16. . . . Qe7) 17. Nd6.

17.	Qd2	axb5
18.	Rxd7	Qxd7!
19.	Qxd7	Bxc3 +

Now White loses the right to castle, and his king becomes particularly vulnerable, especially since he is unable to complete his development.

20.	Ke2	Rfd8

Black has four pieces in play, and White only his queen. With Black also having the attack, White's prospects are seemingly poor.

21.	Qxb7	. . .

After White's 21st move

21.	. . .	Ng5!!

Closing the exit at f3.

22.	e4	Rxa3
23.	Qxb5	Ra2 +
24.	Ke3	. . .

Black played his 24th move and White resigned (0-1).

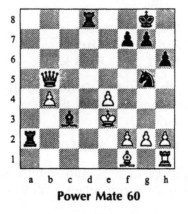

Power Mate 60

Q60: How did Black direct a mating net without a queen?

POWER GAME **61**

Groszpeter vs. C. Horvath
Budapest, 1992

This is warfare at its most bellicose, with White commencing a furious kingside offensive before castling, which he eventually does queenside. Black defends, and though not fully developed, manages to reduce the onslaught by exchanging queens. But it's not enough, and White's momentum is so Newtonian that his inversely proportionate forces gravitate to mate.

Gruenfeld Defense D85

1.	d4	Nf6
2.	c4	g6
3.	Nc3	d5
4.	cxd5	Nxd5
5.	e4	Nxc3
6.	bxc3	Bg7
7.	Bb5 +	...

After White's 7th move

This bishop check was a favorite of East German grand-master R. Knaak in the early 1970s. It faded into oblivion for almost two decades. Then, in 1992 and 1993, it resurfaced with a vengeance. Now, it seems again on the wane.

7.	...	c6
8.	Ba4	b5
9.	Bb3	b4
10.	Qf3	0-0
11.	Ne2	bxc3
12.	h4!?	c5?

Trying to collapse White's center, but here 12. . . . h5! would be better.

13.	h5	cxd4
14.	hxg6	...

After White's 14th move

White's center is gone, but so is the black king's pawn cover.

14.	...	e6

The recapture 14. . . . hxg6 leads fatally to 15. Qg3, threatening 16. Qxg6 or 16. Qh4.

15.	Qh5!	fxg6
16.	Qxh7 +	Kf7

17.	Bh6	Qf6
18.	Bxg7!	Qxg7
19.	Nxd4	Re8
20.	0-0-0	Na6

After Black's 20th move

21.	Rd3!	. . .

The queens are coming off the board, but White still has a mating attack.

21.	. . .	Qxh7
22.	Rxh7 +	Kf6

Or 22. . . . Kf8 23. Rf3+ Kg8 24. Rfh3, with threats to mate or win the rook.

23.	f4	. . .

Threatens 24. e5#. The push 23. . . . e5 permits 24. Rf7#.

23.	. . .	g5
24.	e5 +	Kg6

White played his 25th move and Black resigned (1-0).

Power Mate 61

Q61: How did White construct a mating net?

POWER GAME **62**

Yusupov vs. Timman
Tilburg, 1986

With Mel Gibson–like straightforward aggressiveness, White propels the h-pawn ahead and opens a line for the king-rook. To certify this safely, White closes the center, averting counterattack. Black tries the queenside, abandoning the kingside to White's marauders, which culminate their maneuvers with a breakthrough at h7. The besieged king is deflected, the invader's queen moves in, and Black succumbs when his burdened rook is unable to guard two places at once.

Gruenfeld Defense D86

1.	d4	Nf6
2.	c4	g6
3.	Nc3	d5
4.	cxd5	Nxd5
5.	e4	Nxc3
6.	bxc3	Bg7
7.	Bc4	b6?

After Black's 7th move

The normal line is 7. . . . 0-0 and 8. . . . c5, assailing White's pawn center. The text, an accelerated version of the Simagin Variation (7. . . . 0-0 and 8. . . . b6), delays the assault in favor of developing the queenside pieces.

8.	Qf3	0-0
9.	Ne2	Nc6
10.	h4	. . .

Since Black has refrained from playing c7-c5, White begins an immediate attack on the black castled position.

10.	. . .	Na5
11.	Bd3	e5

If Black does nothing in the center, White's attack will fuel itself.

12.	Ba3	Re8
13.	h5	Qd7!
14.	Rd1	Qa4

Safer would be 14. . . . Qg4.

15.	Bc1	c5?

Allowing White to lock the center. Better would be 15. . . . exd4 16. cxd4 Nc6, keeping White occupied.

16.	d5	Qxa2

After Black's 16th move

| | 17. | Bh6! | Bh8 |

Usually, Black tries to retain his king-bishop, but here
17. . . . Bxh6 18. hxg6 fxg6! 19. Rxh6 Rf8 offers great chances
for resistance. Now Black's king looks cornered.

| 18. | Bb5 | Rd8 |
| 19. | Bg5 | Qb3 |

Black offered the exchange, 20. Bxd8 Qxb5, in hopes of
slowing down White's offensive, but it's too late for pallia-
tive measures.

| 20. | hxg6 | fxg6 |

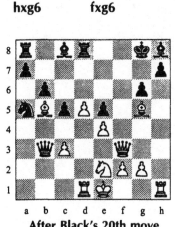

After Black's 20th move

| 21. | Rxh7! | . . . |

Deflecting Black's king away from f7.

21.	. . .	Kxh7
22.	Qf7 +	Bg7
23.	Bf6	Rg8

White played his 24th move and Black resigned (1-0).

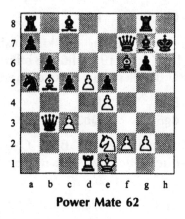

Power Mate 62

Q62: What subtle move did White play to force mate?

POWER GAME **63**

Bareev vs. Kasparov
Paris, 1991

White starts assertively, but Black brushes him off, advantageously trading a wing pawn for one in the middle. To enhance his already prominent position, Black sacrifices the exchange, obtaining terrific piece play, including a radiantly centralized queen and a laterally active rook. When the two suddenly switch their attentions to the same kingside square, White is caught flatfooted and the square dance is over.

Gruenfeld Defense D94

1.	d4	Nf6
2.	c4	g6
3.	Nc3	Bg7
4.	Nf3	0-0
5.	e3	c5
6.	Be2	cxd4
7.	exd4	d5

After Black's 7th move

8.	0-0	Nc6
9.	h3	Bf5
10.	cxd5	Nxd5
11.	Qb3	...

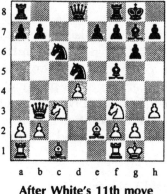

After White's 11th move

White plays a reversed Tarrasch Defense, but the move in hand does not seem to have helped. Black already has the initiative.

11.	...	Be6!

Offering the b-pawn in exchange for White's d-pawn, which here is a great deal.

12.	Qxb7	Nxd4
13.	Nxd4	Bxd4
14.	Bh6	...

If 14. Rd1, Black has 14. . . . Rb8 15. Qa6 Bxc3 16. bxc3 Qc8.

14.	...	Rb8
15.	Qa6	Rxb2

Not only capturing a pawn, but also seizing the seventh rank.

16.	Nxd5	...

White fails after 16. Bxf8 Nxc3, when Black also gains a bishop.

16.	...	Qxd5

After Black's 16th move

Black is losing the exchange, but he gets more than enough in return, including an extra pawn and active pieces.

17.	Bxf8	Kxf8
18.	a4	...

White should let the a-pawn go and secure his position with 18. Bf3. After the text his game collapses.

18.	...	Rb3!

With a threat that White overlooks.

19.	Rad1	...

Nothing really works. If 19. Bf3, then 19. . . . Rxf3 20. gxf3 Qxf3, with a disturbing kingside offensive. Also doomed is 19. Kh1 Rxh3 +, as is 19. Kh2 Bxa1 20. Rxa1 Qe5 +. Black played his 19th move and White resigned (0-1).

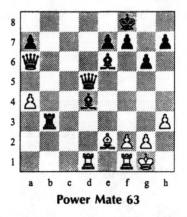

Power Mate 63

Q63: What unexpected quiet move ended White's recalcitrance?

*P*OWER GAME *64*

Kasparov vs. Najdorf
Bogojno, 1982

White obtains a classical pawn center and backs it up appropriately, until the time is ripe for an advancing pawn sacrifice. Maneuvering against Black's queen, he steadily positions his forces against Black's king. Black is constrained to mitigate his condition by exchanging a queen for two rooks. But the situation can't be assuaged. White pricks with a pinning combination, the balloon bursts, and out fizzes checkmate.

Queen's Indian Defense E12

1.	d4	Nf6
2.	c4	e6
3.	Nf3	b6
4.	a3	Bb7
5.	Nc3	d5
6.	cxd5	Nxd5
7.	e3	. . .

After White's 7th move

The old main line, very popular in the early 1980s. White sets about building aligned pawns in the middle.

7.	. . .	Be7
8.	Bb5 +	. . .

Played to induce Black into blocking c6.

8.	. . .	c6
9.	Bd3	Nxc3
10.	bxc3	c5
11.	0-0	Nc6
12.	e4	. . .

White establishes a classical pawn center.

12.	. . .	0-0
13.	Be3	cxd4
14.	cxd4	Rc8
15.	Qe2	Na5
16.	Rfe1	Qd6

After Black's 16th move

White has a big pawn center, but what should he do with it? Kasparov provides the answer: the pawns must advance.

17.	d5	. . .

White advances the d-pawn to gain space and open lines, even though it might cost him a pawn.

17.	. . .	exd5
18.	e5	Qe6
19.	Nd4	. . .

Occupying a powerful transfer post. The knight is now ready to jump to the kingside. Also possible was 19. Ng5 Bxg5 20. Bxg5, with good compensation.

19.	. . .	Qxe5
20.	Nf5	Bf6
21.	Qg4	. . .

After White's 21st move

Threatening 22. Bd4. A mark of all great attackers—Kasparov, Alekhine, Keres—is the ability to shift the queen into action at the right moment.

21.	. . .	Rce8?

This is the wrong rook and it loses. Better would be 21. . . . Rfe8, clearing f8, or 21. . . . Qc3.

22.	Bd2	Qxa1

This exchanges the queen for two rooks but doesn't solve the problem. White still has tremendous pressure against g7. If instead 22. . . . Qc7, then 23. Nh6+ Kh8 24. Rxe8 Rxe8 25. Qf5, winning.

23.	Rxa1	Bxa1
24.	Nxg7	Bxg7

White played his 25th move and Black resigned (1-0).

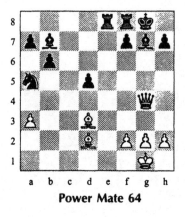

Power Mate 64

Q64: How does White exploit Black's weak kingside to finish with mate?

Malaniuk vs. Danielson
Snekkersten, 1992

It looks as if Black is menacing at first, but it soon dawns that White has turned a defensive situation into counterattack. Instead of lamenting his doubled pawns, he employs them for aggressive advance; and fired by this push, White prepares invasion at h7. Appearances deceive one more time, for Black counts on escaping toward the center, but he's missed a piggish seventh-rank sacrifice, and all is muddied mate.

Queen's Indian Defense E14

1.	d4	Nf6
2.	Nf3	e6
3.	e3	b6
4.	Bd3	Bb7
5.	0-0	Be7
6.	c4	0-0
7.	Nc3	. . .

A quiet line against the Queen's Indian, favored by many top players (Keres, Smyslov, Petrosian, Spassky, Portisch, and Karpov) as they get older. You don't have to know current theory so much. You can just play chess.

7.	. . .	d5
8.	cxd5	. . .

A bit unusual. Normally White retains the central tension with 8. b3. Malaniuk, however, has studied the position and has some points in mind.

8.	. . .	exd5

9.	b3	Nbd7
10.	Bb2	Ne4

After Black's 10th move

11.	Ne2!	. . .

The knight swings around to defend the kingside. At the same time, the diagonal of the queen-bishop is extended, and Nf3-e5 is in the air.

11.	. . .	Bd6
12.	Ng3	Qf6

Stopping both Ne5 and Nf5. Black seems to have a possible kingside attack, but White defends coolly.

13.	Rc1	a6

Prevents Bd3-b5.

14.	Qc2	Nxg3

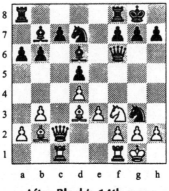

After Black's 14th move

| 15. | hxg3 | . . . |

This obvious capture is best. White has doubled g-pawns, but gets an open h-file. Can he turn this around to his advantage?

| 15. | . . . | Qh6? |

Better is the concrete defense 15. . . . h6; the try 15. . . . g6 leads to a weakening of the long diagonal after 16. e4! dxe4 17. Bxe4.

| 16. | g4! | . . . |

Converting a weakness into a strength. White's liability, the doubled g-pawns, will be used for traumatizing purposes against Black's queen and kingside.

16.	. . .	Rfe8
17.	g3!	Nf8
18.	Kg2	Qe6

Black's queen has to leave the h-file, in view of the impending Rf1-h1.

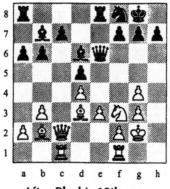

After Black's 18th move

19.	Ng5	Qxg4
20.	Bxh7+	Nxh7
21.	Qxh7+	Kf8

It seems as if Black's king is able to flee to e7. White, however, played his 22nd move and Black resigned (1-0).

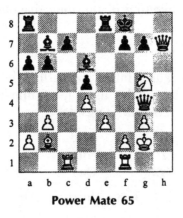

Power Mate 65

Q65: How does White prevent Black's king from escaping forced mate?

Bronstein vs. Geller
Moscow, 1961

The players get to the usual places in a scrimmage, but Black allows White's rook seventh-rank status. It just sits there nonetheless, seemingly unlinked to White's kingside campaign, until White finds an ingenious way to tie everything together. A deflective queen sacrifice is the link uniting all in mating's great chain.

Nimzo-Indian Defense E27

1.	d4	Nf6
2.	c4	e6
3.	Nc3	Bb4
4.	a3	. . .

Fritz Samisch's variation. White obtains the two bishops, a pair of pawns in the center, and attacking chances on the kingside. Black gets easy development and play against White's weakened queenside pawns out of the opening.

4.	. . .	Bxc3 +
5.	bxc3	0-0
6.	f3	d5
7.	cxd5	exd5

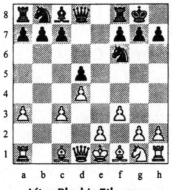

After Black's 7th move

8.	e3	Bf5
9.	Ne2	Nbd7
10.	Nf4	c5
11.	Bd3	Bxd3
12.	Qxd3	Re8
13.	0-0	Rc8

After Black's 13th move

Black seems to have everything under control. He's traded off one of White's bishops and prevented the advance of the e-pawn.

14. Rb1 . . .

A seemingly pure attack on the b-pawn, yet one with far-reaching consequences.

14. . . . Qa5

Geller rejects 14. . . . b6 as too passive, and invites the rook onto b7.

15. Rxb7 . . .

Taking a pawn and the seventh rank simultaneously.

15. . . . Nb6

Geller's idea. The rook is isolated and in danger of being cut off by c5-c4, along with Qa5-a6.

16. g4! . . .

Bronstein's fantastic counter. Is the b7-rook really going to link up with the g-pawn?

16. . . . h6?

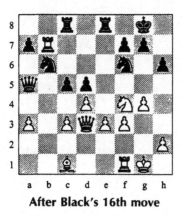

After Black's 16th move

Trying to hold up the g-pawn doesn't work. Nor does 16. . . . c4 because of 17. Qf5 Qa6 18. Rxb6 axb6 19. g5. The right move, found by Kholmov, was 16. . . . g6!, denying access to f5.

	17. h4	cxd4

Since 17. . . . c4 doesn't work, Geller changes his plan and tries to force entry on the c-file.

	18. g5!	. . .

Nothing distracts White from his aim: rolling Black up on the kingside.

	18. . . .	dxe3
	19. gxf6	Rxc3

Black is menacing the white queen, but White replied with his 20th move and Black resigned (**1-0**).

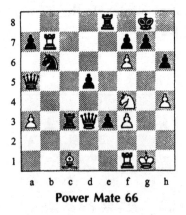

Power Mate 66

Q66: How can White crash through to crush his lofty opponent?

POWER GAME 67

Lyrberg vs. Nielsen
Minsk, 1994

White manufactures a premature attack, which Black incisively refutes. Drawing on sound development, Black's resources are just enough to permit sacrificing the exchange to break the assault. With White's king uncastled and his remaining forces in disarray, he is unable to cope with Black's emerging threats. One deflects the queen, the other dethrones the king.

Nimzo-Indian Defense E29

1.	d4	Nf6
2.	c4	e6
3.	Nc3	Bb4
4.	a3	. . .

The Samisch system. White wants the two bishops and is willing to spend a tempo to get them.

4.	. . .	Bxc3 +
5.	bxc3	0-0
6.	e3	c5
7.	Ne2	Nc6
8.	Ng3	b6
9.	e4	Ne8
10.	Bd3	Ba6
11.	e5	cxd4
12.	cxd4	. . .

After White's 12th move

This has all been seen before. In Pliester-Ligterink, Amsterdam, 1983, Black grabbed the d-pawn, 12. . . . Nxd4, but soon came under a barrage after 13. Bb2 Nc6 14. Qh5.

> **12.   . . .   d5!**

An improvement, mentioned by Sosonko and Pliester in their analysis of the earlier game. White's shaky center is about to collapse.

> **13.   Qh5   f5!**

After Black's 13th move

14.	Nxf5	. . .

A desperate attempt to drum up an attack. After 14. exf6 Nxf6, White is driven back and one of the center pawns is lost.

14.	. . .	exf5
15.	Bxf5	. . .

After White's 15th move

15.	. . .	Rxf5!

Puts an end to the aggression. Now it's Black's turn. How quickly the tables can turn when one is willing to give up material for other kinds of advantage.

16.	Qxf5	Nxd4
17.	Qd3	dxc4
18.	Qe4	Bb7!
19.	Qxb7	. . .

White's queen has been deflected away from the critical area, and now Black played and mated on his 20th move (0-1).

Power Mate 67

Q67: How did Black force a mating check?

*P*OWER GAME *68*

Panzer vs. Wells
Hastings, 1988

White gets too meticulous in preparing central action, weakening the e1-h4 diagonal, which Black promptly exploits. Playing on a fast initiative, Black is able to allow a queen trade without defusing his jet engines. With open b- and d-files for rook transport, Black holidays with a rook sacrifice to visit the seventh rank. White's exposed king and scattered defenses are drenched in bleak mate.

Nimzo-Indian Defense E32

1.	d4	Nf6
2.	c4	e6
3.	Nc3	Bb4
4.	Qc2	0-0
5.	a3	Bxc3 +
6.	Qxc3	b6

After Black's 6th move

A popular position in the Nimzo. Main moves now are 7. Bg5, 7. Nf3, and 7. e3.

	7.	f3	. . .

This is also good if properly followed up.

	7.	. . .	d5
	8.	cxd5?	. . .

A slip. Correct is 8. Bg5.

	8.	. . .	Nxd5!

Attacks White's queen and opens a line for the black queen.

	9.	Qc2	. . .

White decides to let the d-pawn go. The alternative was the self-blocking 8. Qd2, but after 8. . . . f5, White is jammed for space.

	9.	. . .	Qh4 +
	10.	g3	Qxd4
	11.	e4	Ne3!

To foster the attack the knight must go forward, even at the risk of getting trapped.

	12.	Qd3	Ng2 +

After Black's 12th move

| 13. | Kd1 | ... |

On 13. Bxg2?, Black has the simple 13. . . . Qxd3; and on
13. Ke2?, look to 13. . . . Ba6.

13.	...	Qxd3 +
14.	Bxd3	Rd8
15.	Ke2	Nc6
16.	Bc4	...

After White's 16th move

If 16. Be3?, then 16. . . . Rxd3 17. Kxd3 Ba6+ 18. Kd2
Rd8+, followed by Ng2xe3. Yes, Black has a knight check
at d4, but that's answered by moving the king, attacking the
g2-knight. Black has a better way to go.

| 16. | ... | b5! |

The start of a combination to lure White's bishop off the a6-
f1 diagonal.

| 17. | Bxb5 | Rb8! |
| 18. | Bxc6 | ... |

If 18. a4, then 18. . . . Nd4+ 19. Kf2 Ne1 saves the knight;
but 18. a4 is still a better defense than the text.

| 18. | ... | Ba6 + |

19.   Kf2   . . .

The interposition 19. Bb5 causes only momentary interference. After 19. . . . Rxb5 20. Kf2 Rxb2 + !, we're back in the
actual game. Black now played his 19th move and White
resigned (0-1).

Power Mate 68

Q68: How does Black mate with solid backing?

*P*OWER GAME **69**

Stefanov vs. Andreyev
Bulgaria, 1975

White goes queenside with his king, and Black rapidly mobilizes the region. The open a- and b-files become salient, as does the a1-h8 diagonal once Black sacrifices a knight on e4. The definitive boom is lowered by a queen offering at a2, followed by a discovered check that prevents escape. White's futile king is driven up the board, check after check, and disrespectfully mated in the enemy's queenside corner, an outcast from heroism's drama.

King's Indian Defense E81

1.	d4	Nf6
2.	c4	g6
3.	Nc3	Bg7
4.	e4	d6
5.	f3	0-0
6.	Bg5	. . .

After White's 6th move

This has become a popular way to play the Samisch in the 1990s. The standard move for decades was 6. Be3.

6.	...	c5
7.	d5	Qa5
8.	Qd2	...

Also seen these days is 8. Bd2.

| 8. | ... | a6 |
| 9. | 0-0-0 | ... |

After White's 9th move

Castling into it. Almost anything else would be safer: 9. Bd3, 9. Nge2, or 9. h4, for example.

9.	...	b5
10.	cxb5	axb5
11.	Bxb5	Ba6
12.	Ba4	Nxe4?!

Black is caught in the spirit of attack and begins to sacrifice. This pays off later on, but at the moment this offering is suspect.

| 13. | Nxe4? | ... |

Correct is 13. fxe4 Bxc3 14. Qxc3 Qxa4 15. Bh6.

13.	...	Qxa4
14.	Kb1?	...

After White's 14th move

This doesn't help matters, but White is in horrific trouble in any event.

	14.	...	Qxa2 + !!

A spectacular shot. A quieter method would be 13. . . . Bd3+ 14. Kc1 (or 14. Qxd3 Qxa2+ and 15. . . . Qxb2#) 14. . . . Qxa2 15. Qf2 Bd4, winning.

15.	Kxa2	Bd3 +
16.	Kb3	c4 +

Inducing White's king to walk the plank.

17.	Kb4	Na6 +
18.	Kb5	Rfb8 +

The king hunt proceeds.

19.	Kc6	Rc8 +
20.	Kb7	...

The longest mate is 20, Kb5 (instead of 20. Kb7) 20. . . . Nc7+ 21. Kc6 Ne6+ 22. Kb7 Rcb8+ 23. Kc6 Nd8+ 24. Kd7 Rb7+ 25. Ke8 Ne6#. The shortest? Who knows?

20.	...	Rc7 +!
21.	Kxa8	...

Black played his 21st move and White resigned (0-1).

Power Mate 69

Q69: What quiet move announced the mate?

Sakins vs. Dambitis
Lithuania (correspondence), 1978

Each side advances pawns to gain space and push the attack: White in the center, and Black on the kingside. But White takes a tempo to scare away Black's frightening knight, and it costs him, for Black sacrifices it on f2. White's king must take back and is caught in a king chase. Yelping all the way to the queenside, he is hunted down like a dog and mated.

King's Indian Defense E93

1.	d4	Nf6
2.	c4	g6
3.	Nc3	Bg7
4.	e4	d6
5.	Nf3	0-0
6.	Be2	e5
7.	d5	Nbd7
8.	Be3	...

The old move is 8. Qc2, replaced by Petrosian's 8. Bg5. The text move is hardly ever played in this position.

8.	...	Ng4

Attacking the e3-bishop and gaining time to advance the f-pawn.

9.	Bd2	...

A possible improvement would be 9. Bg5 f6 10. Bh4.

9.	...	f5!
10.	h3?	...

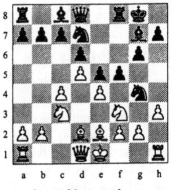

After White's 10th move

Now 10. Ng5 is the best chance.

10.	. . .	Nxf2!
11.	Kxf2	fxe4
12.	Nxe4	. . .

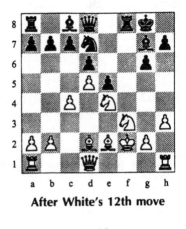

After White's 12th move

12.	. . .	Qh4 +
13.	Ke3	. . .

If 13. Ng3, Black has 13. . . . Nc5!, which threatens Nc5-e4 + as well as e5-e4.

13.	. . .	Bh6 +
14.	Kd3	Qxe4 +!
15.	Kc3	. . .

After White's 15th move

Take the queen on e4, 15. Kxe4, and be silenced by 15. . . . Nc5#.

15.	. . .	Bg7!
16.	Rf1	. . .

If White tries to trap Black's queen with 16. Bd3, Black counters with 16. . . . Rxf3! 17. Qxf3 Qd4 +, followed by e5-e4.

16.	. . .	Nc5
17.	b4	Rxf3 +
18.	gxf3	. . .

Or 18. Rxf3 Qd4 + 19. Kc2 e4. Black played his 18th move and White resigned (**0-1**).

Power Mate 70

Q70: How is Black's mate achieved?

ANSWERS

1 It's mate after **18. . . . Qh6+ 19. Kg4** (if 19. Bh5, then 19. . . . Qxh5#) **19. . . . f5+! 20. Kxf5 Qg6#**, a neat criss-cross mate of queen and bishop, and not even the *Rachel* can save White's king from drowning.

2 The likely conclusion is **18. . . . Bxg4+ 19. Kc1** (if 19. Be2 then Qh1# is a pin-mate) **19. . . . Qe1+ 20. Qd1 Qxd1#**.

3 Black played **19. . . . Nb4+**, and White resigned, for nothing can stop mate: **(A) 20. axb4 Qd3#**, a swallow's tail mate; or **(B) 20. Kb1 Qd3#**, also a swallow's tail mate.

4 The basic concluding line is **22. fxg4 Nh4** and mate follows on g2. In the event of 22. Qd6, Sax gives 22. . . . Nf4, which compels 23. Qxf4. But there's a problem-like finish with **22. . . . Rf4!**, obstructing the b8-h2 diagonal. It forces mate: **(A) 23. Qxf4 Nxf4** and mate on g2 or h2; **(B) 23. exf4 Qxh2#**; **(C) 23. fxg4 Nh4 24. Bf3 Nxf3+**, or even **24. . . . Qxf3**.

5 Black forged ahead with **24. . . . Bd4+**, and White resigned, for it's mate via **25. Kf1 Qf2#**.

6 White made Black resign by **24. Qd8+**. See for yourself; it's mate after **24. . . . Kg7 25. Qxg5+ Kf8 26. Rd8#**.

This game bears a number of similarities to the best-known chess game ever played, Paul Morphy vs. the Duke of Brunswick and Count Isouard, played at a Paris opera house in 1858. The parallels include: (1) a minor piece sacrifice for Black's b- and c-pawns; (2) the move Bxd7+, followed by Qb8+; (3) a diagonal check from b5; (4) pile-up on a pinned d7-rook; and (5) mate on d8 with a rook, supported by a diagonal piece from g5.

7 Black calls it quits before 21. . . . Kg6 22. f5+! Kh7 (22. . . . Kh6 is answered by 23. Qxh8#) 23. Ng5+ Kh6 24. Qf6#.

8 White continued with **24. Bf6! Bxf6 25. exf6**, and Black resigned, there being no way to avert a queen support mate at g7. This pattern is also known as Lolli's Mate.

9 White deflected with **24. Rh7+!**, and Black gave up. The anticipated 24. . . . Kxh7 25. Qxf7+ Kh6 (25. . . . Kh8 also ends in mate after 26. Rh1+) 26. Rh1+ Bh5 concretizes in 27. Rxh5#. Moreover, the fruitless 24. . . . Kg6 (or 24. . . . Kg8 or 24. . . . Kf8) is dispensed with by 25. Qxf7#.

10 Black mated by **21. . . . g5+ 22. Kh5 Qh3+ 23. Kxg5 Be3+ 24. Kf6 Qe6#**.

11 A rook lift!—**21. Re3!** Even 21. . . . Bf4 can't prevent eventual mate: 22. Rh3+ Bh6 23. Bxh6 gxh6 24. Rxh6#. This idea is reminiscent of the conclusion to Alekhine-Lasker, Zurich, 1934.

12 White's knightish conclusion was **20. Nd6+ Kd8 21. Qe8+!**, when 21. . . . Nxe8 22. Nf7# is a semi-smothered mate (the e6-pawn is needed to guard a square).

13 Black resigned after **16. Ng5+ Ke8 17. Qe6+**. There are two tricky Tal mates: 17. . . . Kd8 18. Nf7+ Kc7 19. Qd6#; and 17. . . . Ne7 18. Qf7+ Kd8 19. Ne6#.

14 Mate by **20. Bf7#** comes to mind.

15 Black resigned after **19. Nxg6+ hxg6 20. Rxh5+** when 20. . . . gxh5 21. Qxh5+ Bh6 22. Qxh6# sounds the game's coda.

16 It was over after **18. Qc7+**. Black resigned rather than be mated linearly: 18. . . . Ke8 19. Qxc8+ Rxc8 20. Rxc8#.

17 After **25. Qxh6+!**, Black gave up. You can track the mate by playing out 25. . . . Bxh6 26. Rxh6+ Kg7 27. Rh7+ Kxf6 28. Rxf8#.

18 White stopped the agony with **25. Rxh7+**, and Black resigned, for 25. . . . Kxh7 26. Qh4+ Kg7 27. Qh6# completes the encirclement.

19 With **22. Rxh6+!** Black was forced to resign, for it's mate by 22. . . . Kxh6 23. Qg6#.

20 Mate was commenced by **23. Qg4+**, when Black resigned rather than face 23. . . . Bg7 24. Bxf6 and 25. Qxg7# (23. . . . Kh8 is met by 24. Bxf6+ Bg7 25. Qxg7#).

21 Mate is achieved by **25. Qxh7+!!** The end would be 22. . . . Kxh7 23. Rh3+ Kg7 24. Bh6+ Kh8 25. Bf8+ Nh4 26. Rxh4#.

22 There are mates all over the place:

(A) 25. . . . Qxe6 26. Qc7+ Qd7 27. Bd6# (primary); or 26. . . . Kf8 27. Bd6+ Re7 (27. . . . Qxd6 28. Qf7#) 28. Qd8+ Kf7 29. Qxe7#; or 27. . . . Qe7 (now mate becomes a real problem) 28. Bc5 (threat of 29. Qf4+) 28. . . . Bf6 (28. . . . Be5 29. Qxe5 Rg7 30. Qf6+ Rf7 31. Qxf7# or 31. Qh8#) 29. gxf6 Rg7 (else 30. Bxe7+, etc.) 30. fxe7+ Rgxe7 (30. . . . Rexe7 31. Qd8#) 31. Qe5! and mate next move.

(B) 25. . . . Kf7 26. Rf6+ Ke7 27. Rf7#.

(C) 25. . . . Kf8 26. Rxe8+ Qxe8 28. Bd6#. And who knows? Maybe there are more.

23 White stopped the show with **24. Rxf7+!**, and it's mate however Black replies: if 24. . . . Kxf7, then 25. Qxe6#; or if 24. . . . Rxf7, then 25. Rxe6#.

24 White forced mate by **24. Qg7+!**, when 24. . . . Kxg7 25. Nf5+ (double check) Kg8 26. Nh6# is a beautiful bishop-and-knight mate.

25 Black immediately gave up after **17. Qxf8+!**, unable to forestall mate by 17. . . . Kxf8 18. Bh6+ Kg8 19. Re8#. This game, by the way, is a move-for-move repeat of Livchenkov-Eganian, USSR, 1979.

26 The remarkable finish is **23. Qe8+**, when 23. . . . Kg7 is flattened by 24. Nf5#—a beautiful pattern!

27 The game stopped after **20. Qh5!** If 20. . . . Qxh5 (20. . . . f6 allows 21. Ne7#), then 21. Ne7+ Kh7 22. Rxh5#.

28 The winning rejoinder is **23. Be4!**, when Black's queen is overloaded, unable to capture on e4 without abandoning control of f6. If 23. . . . Qxe4 (else 24. Qxh7#), then 4. Qxf6+ Kg8 25. Qg7#.

29 It's mate after 26. Rxg6+ fxg6 27. Qxg6+ and 28. Qg7#.

30 Mate follows no matter how Black replies. If 25. . . . Nxe8 (or 25. . . . Rxe8 26. Qb4+ Kg8 27. dxe8/Q+ Nxe8 28. Ne7+ Kf8 29. Ng6+ Kg8 30. Qf8#—), then 26. Qb4+ Nd6 27. Qxd6+ Kg8 28. Ne7+ Kf8 29. Ng6+ Kg8 30. Qf8+ Rxf8 31. Ne7# is a smothered mate.

31 The definitive **17. gxh7#,** a gorgeous pawn finish, was White's reply.

32 White's potent rook lift prepared Black's entombment by **26. Rh3.** If 25. . . . exd4, the game terminates after 26. Rh3 Qe5 27. Rh8+ (a clearance sac) Bxh8 28. Qh7#.

33 White's trick was **22. Rxh8+! Kxh8 23. Bxf6+,** when Black resigned rather than disappear by 23. . . . exf6 24. Qh6+ Kg8 25. Rh1, which renders mate at h8 enchantingly.

34 The game was over after **19. Qxg7+!! Kxg7 20. Rg6#,** a model discovered mate.

35 There is no stopping 23. Qg7+ Bxg7 24. hxg7+ Kg8 25. Rh8#.

36 White continued funereally with **22. Ng8+,** to which Black responded **22. . . . Ke8,** allowing **23. Bxf7+ Kf8 24. Rd8+** and mate next move. On 22. . . . Kf8, there would have followed the solemn 23. Rxf7+ Ke8 24. Rf6#; if 22. . . . Rxg8, then the gloomy conclusion is 23. Rxf7+ Ke8 24. Rc7+ Kf8 25. Rd8+ Qe8 26. Rxe8# (or 26. Rf7#).

37 Mate materializes on h1 after **19. . . . Qh1+!** (White resigned) 20. Bxh1 Rxh1#. Apparently White missed this x-ray support for h1.

38 The knockout was achieved with the blow **21. Rxg7+!,** and Black gave up, for 21. . . . Kxg7 22. f6+ Qxf6 allows mate at h7. In fact, mate at h7 is guaranteed.

39 Black's resignation was forced by **15. Qa5+,** when 15. . . . b6 is mated by either 16. Qxb6+ axb6 17. Bxb6# or 16. Bxb6+ axb6 17. Qxb6#.

40 Everything is transparent with **17. Qxh7 +** ! Black resigned here, seeing how after 17. . . . Kxh7 18. Rh4 + Kg8 19. Rh8#, it's illegal for him to play another move.

41 The mate follows straightforwardly: 24. Kb4 Qe7 + 25. Kb3 Qe6 + 26. Kb4 Qc4 + 27. Ka5 Qc5#.

42 White closed down the show with **12. Bg5 +** ! If 12. . . . Ne7, then 13. Qxe7#. Everything else allows 13. Nxf7#, mainly because of the interference block.

43 A Morphy-like game. It would have consummated 20. . . . Kf7 21. Qh7 + Kf8 (or 21. . . . Ke6 22. Qg8 + Ke5 23. Qd5# or 22. . . . Ke7 23. Qe8#) 22. Qg8 + Ke7 23. Qe8#.

44 Black forced White's resignation by **15. . . . Qxf3 +** !, for it's mate next move: either 16. gxf3 Bh3# (a criss-cross bishop mate) or 16. Qf2 Qxf2# (a support mate).

45 White finished with **21. Bg6 +** , which would end either by 21. . . . Kg8 22. Qf7 + Kh8 23. Qh7#, or 21. . . . Kh6 22. Bf5 + Kh5 23. g4#.

46 The game was ended neatly by **17. . . . Qh2 +** !! **18. Bxh2 Nf2#** !

47 Black missed the threat completely, which was to force mate by a deflecting queen sacrifice **22. Qxf8 +** ! The game concluded in a bishop-and-knight mate after **22. . . . Rxf8 23. Ne7#**.

48 White forced Black to give up by **11. Nh6!**, for 11. . . . gxh6 permits 12. Bxh6#. Otherwise, White's queen is supported for mate at either f7 or g8.

49 Black finished matters with **13. . . . Ng4,** and White gave up, unable to cope with the mate threat at h2. If 14. Nxg4, for example, then he gets mated at g2, 14. . . . Qg2#.

50 Black resigned after **22. Rxf7 + Kd8** (22 . . . Ke623. Qh3 +) **23. Rd7 +.** The game should then conclude with 23. . . . Kc8 24. Rc7 + Kb8 (or 24. . . . Kd8 25. Qd7#) 25. Rxb7 + Kc8 26. Qd7# (or 26. Qc7#).

51 The winner was **17. Qc6!!,** and it's glorious mate after 17. . . . bxc6 18. bxc6 Kb8 19. Rfa1, when any 19th move for Black results in 20. Ra8#. After the game, 16. . . . Nf6 (instead of 16. . . . Kc8) was suggested as a better defense. The idea is to meet 17. Rfa1 with 17. . . . Kc8 18. Qc6 bxc6 19. bxc6 Nd7 20. Ra8 + Nb8. But even here, 21. R1a7, followed by Rb7, is convincing.

52 He started with **19. Nf5 + !** After 19. . . . Bxf5 20. Rh4 + (note the g-pawn is pinned and can't capture the rook) 20. . . . Nh5, it's mate by 21. Rxh5 +.

53 The sunburst **23. . . . Bxh2 +** ends it in mate: 24. Nxh2 Qg6 + 25. Kf1 (or 25. Ng4 Qxg4 +) 25. . . . Qg2#.

54 Mate is forced by **14. Qa7 + Kxb5 15. a4 +,** when 15. . . . Kb4 is met by 16. Qb6#.

55 Mate follows after **24. . . . Rh1 + !,** when 25. Kxh1 Rh8 + 26. Kg1 Rh1 + ! 27. Kxh1 Qh8 + 28. Kg1 Qh2# does the trick; or 28. Bh6 Qxh6 + 29. Kg1 Qh2#.

56 After **24. Bc5 + !** Rxc5, the only move, White mates by the invasive 25. Ng8#!—great two-knight action.

57 After the intrusion **17. Qh7+**, Black had no choice but to resign, since 16. . . . Kf8 17. Bd6+ forces a block at e7, with a queen mate to follow at h8.

58 White put the final period in with **24. Qxg6!!**, threatening 25. Qh7#. If 24. . . . hxg5, then 25. Nf6+ Kh8 26. Qh7#. And if the queen is captured, 24. . . . fxg6, then it's over after 25. Ne7+ Kh8 26. Nxg6#. The best that Black can do is sac a few pieces to delay inevitable mate.

59 It's mate after **25. Qd5+** Kc7 26. Re7+ Kb6 27. Qb7#.

60 Black began the end with **24. . . . Bd2+!** After 25. Ke2, the discovery 25. . . . Bf4+ results in 26. Ke1 Ra1+ 27. Ke2 Rd2#—great coordinated use of the little pieces!

61 The mating net was set up by **25. Rdh3**. After 25. . . . gxf4 26. Bc2+ Kg5, it ends with 27. Rg7#.

62 The intrusive **24. Be8!** leads to mate. A possible conclusion is 24. . . . Bf5 (to guard g6) 25. exf5 Raxe8 26. Qxg6+ Kh8 27. Qh6#.

63 Black terminated his opponent by **19. . . . Rg3!**, when the rook can't be captured because of the pin on the f2-pawn. And if 20. Bf3, then 19. . . . Qxf3, with the same unpreventable mate at g2.

64 After **25. Bh6**, mate on g7 is unavoidable.

65 White wins with **22. Rxc7!**, taking control of e7 and threatening Qh7-h8#. If 22. . . . Bxc7, White scores with 23. Ba3+; and if 23. . . . Re7, then 24. Qh8#.

66 White answers with the incredible **20. Qg6!!**, and mate is as certain as taxes. If **20. . . . fxg6**, then **21. Rxg7+ Kh8** (or **21. . . . Kf8**). **22. Nxg6#**. Otherwise, White simply mates on g7 with his queen.

67 The game ended suddenly and dramatically with **19. . . . Nc2+ 20. Ke2 Qd3#!** Note that on **20. Kf1**, Black still has mate by **20. . . . Qd1#**.

68 Black wins with the capturing deflection **19. . . . Rxb2+!**, when **20. Bxb2 Rd2+ 21. Ne2 Rxe2+** leads to mate. If **22. Kg1**, then **22. . . . Ne3** followed by **Re2-g2#** concludes.

69 With **21. . . . Bd4!**, it was clear that Armageddon was on the way, for **Rc7-a7#** is unstoppable.

70 White resigned after **18. . . . Qd4+**, when mate is ordained by **19. Kc2 Bf5+ 20. Bd3 Bxd3+ 21. Kc1 Qxa1#**.

ECO Codes and Descriptive Openings Index

CLASSIFICATION OF OPENINGS BY GROUP

OPENINGS: CODES AND DESCRIPTIVE NAMES

A50	Old Queen's Indian Defense
A51–52	Budapest Counter Gambit
A53–55	Old Indian Defense
A56	Czech Benoni Defense
A57–59	Benko Gambit
A60–79	Modern Benoni Defense
A80–99	Dutch Defense
B00	Nimzovich Defense
B01	Center Counter Defense
B02–05	Alekhine Defense
B06–09	Modern/Pirc Defense
B10–19	Caro-Kann Defense
B20–99	Sicilian Defense
C00–19	French Defense
C20	Alapin Opening
C21	Danish Gambit
C22	Center Game
C23–24	Bishop's Opening
C25–29	Vienna Game
C30–39	King's Gambit
C40	Latvian Counter Gambit
C41	Philidor Defense
C42–43	Petrov Defense
C44	Ponziani Opening/Scotch Gambit
C45	Scotch Game
C46	Three Knights Game
C47	Scotch Game
C48–49	Four Knights Game
C50–59	Italian Game (Giuoco Piano)
C60–99	Ruy Lopez

Index

About the Author

BRUCE PANDOLFINI is the author of seventeen instructional chess books, including *The Chess Doctor; Chess Thinking; Chess Target Practice; More Chess Openings: Traps and Zaps 2; Beginning Chess; Pandolfini's Chess Complete; Chessercizes; More Chessercizes; Checkmate!; Principles of the New Chess; Pandolfini's Endgame Course; Russian Chess; The ABC's of Chess; Let's Play Chess; Kasparov's Winning Chess Tactics; One-Move Chess by the Champions; Chess Openings: Traps and Zaps; Square One;* and *Weapons of Chess.* He is also the editor of the distinguished anthologies *The Best of Chess Life & Review,* Volumes I and II, and has produced, with David MacEnuity, two instructional videotapes, *Understanding Chess* and *Opening Principles.*

Bruce was the chief commentator at the New York half of the 1990 Kasparov-Karpov World Chess Championship, and in 1990 was head coach of the United States Team in the World Youth Chess Championships in Wisconsin. Perhaps the most experienced chess teacher in North America, he is co-founder, with Faneuil Adams, of the Manhattan Chess Club School and is the director of the New York City Schools Program. Bruce's most famous student, six-time National Scholastic Champion Joshua Waitzkin, is the subject of Fred Waitzkin's acclaimed book *Searching for Bobby Fischer* and of the movie of the same name. Bruce Pandolfini lives in New York City.